Praise for *The Power of Disability*

"*The Power of Disability* celebrates the way people with disabilities can change the world—not in spite of their disability but because of it. It spoke deeply to me because I have a disability called depression. I don't know how I came through three major bouts with this mental illness and lived to tell the tale. But I do know this: when you've had such an experience, you want to make meaning of it by sharing hope with others who suffer. This book is filled with the stories of many kinds of 'wounded healers,' told wonderfully well by Al Etmanski. I'm very grateful to the author and all whose stories he tells for reminding me, once again, of the power to be found in the places where we feel most vulnerable."

—**Parker J. Palmer, author of *On the Brink of Everything*, *Let Your Life Speak*, and *Healing the Heart of Democracy***

"This book challenges the dominant discourse that persons with disabilities are incapable by focusing on their collective achievements. It is well researched and full of many moving stories of people who have made a difference despite the structural barriers and inequities they faced."

—**Catalina Devandas, UN Special Rapporteur on the Rights of Persons with Disabilities**

"In a world defined by accelerating change and interconnection, those who recognize their differences and give themselves permission to make a difference have a powerful advantage. The stories in this book illustrate how people with disabilities are seizing their power. They will help all of us see and seize ours."

—**Bill Drayton, CEO, Ashoka**

"This is a landmark book. It opens the door to a vibrant world we hardly know and seldom think about—the world of disability—and reveals disability to be the invisible force that has shaped the world. Yes, there is power in disability. There is also wisdom, passion, and practical advice for navigating the turbulent times we live in. *The Power of Disability* is an instruction manual for becoming truly human and a manifesto for transcending all our differences and creating a world where everyone thrives. The stories are readable and highly compelling, suitable for young and old. There should be copies in every school and business on the planet."

—**Caroline Casey, founder of The Valuable 500, disability activist, inclusion advocate**

"I know Al from two contexts: as a thinking partner for our overlapping work on social change and as a family friend when my beautiful grandson Sinai was born with Down syndrome. This brilliant book shows us Al at his best: incisive, humble, loving, tenacious, practical. He helps us all recognize and reach for what is best in the world."

—**Adam Kahane, Director, Reos Partners, and author of *Collaborating with the Enemy* and *Power and Love***

"This book is a who's who of fascinating people who say adapting to disability— their own or that of a loved one—is a wellspring of their creativity and ability to think flexibly. It will change the way you see the world."

—**Louise Kinross, *BLOOM* Editor and Special Projects Manager, Holland Bloorview Kids Rehabilitation Hospital**

"*The Power of Disability* invites us to examine how the lives of people with disabilities can and should be more integrated into the regular flow of society. The book is informative and introduces practical ways for us to engage in conversation about disability in ways that bring us all together as humans. It's a one-of-a-kind read."

—**Steve Hanamura, President, Hanamura Consulting**

"Al Etmanski is a master storyteller. This book is fun to read, inspiring, and filled with a remarkable wisdom for everyday life. Reading it will make you a better caregiver and a better leader and most importantly will compel you to be a better person."

—**Paul Born, Co-CEO, Tamarack Institute**

The Power
of Disability

THE POWER OF DISABILITY

AL ETMANSKI

10 LESSONS FOR SURVIVING, THRIVING, AND CHANGING THE WORLD

BK

Berrett–Koehler Publishers, Inc.

Berrett-Koehler Publishers, Inc.
1333 Broadway, Suite 1000
Oakland, CA 94612-1921
Tel: (510) 817-2277
Fax: (510) 817-2278
www.bkconnection.com

ORDERING INFORMATION

Quantity sales. Special discounts are available on quantity purchases by corporations, associations, and others. For details, contact the "Special Sales Department" at the Berrett-Koehler address above.

Individual sales. Berrett-Koehler publications are available through most bookstores. They can also be ordered directly from Berrett-Koehler: Tel: (800) 929-2929; Fax: (802) 864-7626; www.bkconnection.com.

Orders for college textbook / course adoption use. Please contact Berrett-Koehler: Tel: (800) 929-2929; Fax: (802) 864-7626.

Distributed to the U.S. trade and internationally by Penguin Random House Publisher Services.

Berrett-Koehler and the BK logo are registered trademarks of Berrett-Koehler Publishers, Inc.

Printed in the United States of America.

Berrett-Koehler books are printed on long-lasting acid-free paper. When it is available, we choose paper that has been manufactured by environmentally responsible processes. These may include using trees grown in sustainable forests, incorporating recycled paper, minimizing chlorine in bleaching, or recycling the energy produced at the paper mill.

Library of Congress Cataloging-in-Publication Data
Names: Etmanski, Al, 1947– author.
Title: The power of disability : 10 lessons for surviving, thriving, and
    changing the world / Al Etmanski.
Description: First edition. | Oakland, CA : Berrett-Koehler Publishers,
    [2020] | Includes bibliographical references and index.
Identifiers: LCCN 2019030585 | ISBN 9781523087563 (paperback) |
    ISBN 9781523087570 (pdf) | ISBN 9781523087587 (epub)
Subjects: LCSH: People with disabilities—Social conditions. | Disability
    awareness. | Resilience (Personality trait)
Classification: LCC HV1568.E86 2020 | DDC 305.9/08—dc23
LC record available at https://lccn.loc.gov/2019030585

First Edition

28 27 26 25 24 23 22 21 20 19   10 9 8 7 6 5 4 3 2 1

Cover designer: Peggy Archambault   *Cover Art:* istock image
Back Cover Photos: Cindy Hughes   *Book producer and text designer:* Leigh McLellan Design
Copyeditor: Karen Seriguchi   *Indexer:* Ken DellaPenta

❦

Contents

Lesson 8   Awaken to All Your Senses   115

Lesson 9   Nothing about Us without Us   129

To Anderson

Preface

THERE IS A pretty good chance you are directly or indirectly connected to the power of disability. The majority of people are. For
starters, one-seventh of the people on the planet have a disability, which
makes people with disabilities the largest minority group in the world.
When you factor in their family, friends, and allies, which I conserva-
tively estimate as another three in seven, the disability community
comprises four-sevenths of the world's population.

What you might not know is the full extent of the collective achieve-
ment of people with disabilities.

That's because the history books have largely ignored them, aside
from notable exceptions like Beethoven, Helen Keller, Stephen Hawking, and Temple Grandin. Or credit has been given to someone else.
That's why I have written this book. The time has come to recognize
people with disabilities for who they really are: authoritative sources on
creativity, resilience, love, resistance, dealing with adversity, and living
a good life.

As you are about to read, people with disabilities have been instrumental in the growth of freedom and the birth of democracy. They have
produced heavenly music and exquisite works of art. They have de-
lighted children and the young at heart with some of the most popular
stories ever written. They have made us laugh, touched our souls, and
taught us how to love. They have unveiled the secrets of the universe.
And they have been on the front lines fighting for justice.

They are still doing all those things and more.

This book has two audiences. The first is those who haven't given
people with disability much thought, other than to be inspired by the

occasional feel-good story. Before my daughter Liz was born with her disability, I was in this category. I would like this book to enrich your life the way the disability community has enriched mine.

The second audience is people in the disability community. I would like this book to bring us together and to make disability a greater force to be reckoned with.

The Power of Disability is designed to be a source of everyday wisdom for the everyday reader. Each of the ten lessons in the book has a short explanation of why I chose it, followed by multiple real-life stories, many of them about people you know. These are sprinkled with quotations and "Did You Know . . ." facts. Each profile is a bite-sized chunk of a well-rounded and fascinating life.

My hope is that after reading this book, you will help rewrite history and change the conversation about disability.

The Disability Advantage

The world is like a big round ball.
What bounces the world?

—LIZ ETMANSKI

THIS ISN'T REALLY a book about disability. It's a book about life: Where it comes from. How to live it. Savor it. Celebrate it. And make it better. It contains a treasure chest of good judgment, clear thinking, and street smarts that can help you survive and thrive whatever your trials and tribulations—and, if necessary, change the conditions that created them. The big difference between this book and other social-change, management, and self-help books is that the stories and lessons come from an untapped and underappreciated source, people in the disability community. Here is one of my lessons:

If I could have stopped it, I would have.

She strode onto the stage as cool as a cucumber. Without notes. Without preparation. Seemingly without a care.

A hundred pairs of eyes were watching and waiting.

A recipe for disaster.

A disaster I had tried to prevent from the moment she was born.

It was the scene of my undoing.

"Hey, everybody. Before I begin, I'd like to tell you a little about myself. My name is Liz. I'm an artist, a poet, and I have Down syndrome. What that means is that it takes me a little longer to learn some things. Sometimes.

"OK . . . enough about me."

She snapped her fingers.

The jazz guitarist who sat behind her picked up the beat.

She began, snatching from her memory words and fragments of conversation she had absorbed throughout the conference. She served them back as spoken word poetry. The crowd cheered in recognition. She beamed.

Her confidence shook me open, exposing my lack of confidence. Was it in my daughter's ability to live up to my idea of her? Or worse— in the daughter I had? This daughter who swaggered. Whose taste in clothes, tattoos, and men I hadn't always liked. Who lived by herself in a place that could have been a lot cleaner, with a closet she turned into a studio. And who was more than getting by. Without me. Despite me.

What was I supposed to do now?

I spent many hours when Liz was first born searching for a cure for Down syndrome. I read an article by a doctor who claimed that Down syndrome could be cured with megavitamins. I wanted the formula. I wrote him letters (these were the pre-internet days), tracking him throughout the Midwest to New York, then across the ocean to Glasgow and finally to Stockholm, where his trail evaporated, along with his credentials and my hope in miracles.

After that, I became a zealot for anything that would help Liz fit in. I reasoned that the more she looked and acted like everybody else, the easier her life would be. I bought her expensive clothing with designer labels—anything that would make her acceptable to her peers. I was trying to make her normal, something I had never considered necessary for my other children.

I suppose some good can come from searching for a cure. But not if you miss the true miracle of becoming—of becoming who you are, not someone else's version. Some good can probably come from conforming in some things and at some times. But not if it distracts a dad from the blossoming of his daughter's character.

Since then, I've asked myself why I thought my beautiful and precious baby daughter needed to be fixed. Part of the answer is personal. I was a driven idealist who pursued perfection at all costs in my personal and work lives. I strived to be strong in everything I did. I was impatient if others didn't measure up. To be blunt, I was indifferent to people with disabilities, although I didn't mind helping out those I met. I couldn't understand why some of my university classmates were so keen to pursue a career in the disability field. I wince when I think of the hard-hearted person I was back then.

I have also come to appreciate that I was under the influence of inaccurate stereotypes about people with disabilities. You are probably familiar with some of them: People with disabilities as childish innocents and eternal children, or endowed with superpowers sent to save and amaze us. People with disabilities as Frankenstein-like menaces, unlovable and dangerous, best kept separate from society for their safety and ours. I'm guessing you can think of movies and pictures that reinforce these stereotypes. The doctor who delivered Liz and who told Liz's mom and me that he had bad news for us was under the same influence. So were the nurses and social workers at the hospital who asked us whether we would be bringing her home with us or giving her up to foster care. Imagine asking new parents such a question. Sadly, it still happens.

Even though the representation is getting better, it is still uneven. I recall when Kevin McHale, who played the character Artie Abrams in the television show *Glee* got up from his wheelchair in a dream sequence and began to dance. I was so disappointed. That would not have happened if the actor had actually used a wheelchair. We lost a chance to be introduced to the elegance of wheelchair dancing and were left with the mistaken impression that every person with a disability dreams of not being disabled. By contrast, Lauren Potter played her *Glee* character, the cheerleader Becky Jackson, in a feisty and convincing way. Without doubt that's because both she and her character experienced Down syndrome.

After Liz was born, I became a full-time disability advocate. I used my community-organizing skills to help close institutions and segregated schools for people with developmental disabilities. We blocked roads and took government to court. We also used the courts to establish the right of people with severe disabilities to receive medical treatment. I learned that broad-based coalitions that attracted public support were necessary to get politicians to make bold political decisions. Some of my other involvements include establishing one of the world's first Family Support Institutes for parents of children with disabilities and securing the funds for a five-year national dialogue on redefining citizenship from the perspective of people with disabilities.

In 1989, my wife, Vickie Cammack, and I cofounded Planned Lifetime Advocacy Network (PLAN) to help families answer the question: What happens to their sons and daughters with a disability when the parents die? PLAN does this by creating networks of friends and by developing wills, trusts, and estate plans that protect the wealth of people with disabilities from government encroachment. The PLAN model has spread to more than forty locations around the world. While at PLAN, I proposed and led an antipoverty campaign to create the world's first savings plan for people with disabilities. The collective individual deposits now total more than $4 billion. They can be used on whatever the person wants and can't be clawed back by the government.

Along the way, I began collecting stories, articles, and anecdotes about people with disabilities—anything that would help me understand the daughter I was getting to know and the disability movement that had welcomed me. I found gems of insight in the usual places—newspapers, magazines, books, movies, and television. Nowadays I also find them in blogs, podcasts, YouTube videos, TED Talks, concerts, sporting events, art galleries, songs, Instagram, and Twitter. They were everywhere, once I started looking.

I discovered that people with disabilities have been major players throughout history. If you were to take away their contributions, you wouldn't recognize the world. It would be a much different place and in much rougher shape, even though the history books have missed most of these achievements or have given credit to someone else. I also discovered a debt unpaid. People with disabilities have given the world far more than the world has given them. They have made their contributions throughout history while contending with mistreatment, neglect, and terrible atrocities. They have had to fight for every ounce of support and opportunity in order to survive, let alone thrive and change the world. That's at the best of times. At the worst of times, people with disabilities have been sterilized, locked up, and killed. Few people realize that the Nazis practiced their mass killing methods on people with disabilities first.

The good news is that the golden age of the disability movement is approaching. And it couldn't come soon enough, because the advantages that people with a disability offer, and there are many, are the perfect remedy for the troubled times we live in. The movement includes people whose disability is related to their mobility, mental health, sight, hearing, flexibility, memory, or intellectual development. I describe this in more detail in "A Word about Words." It also includes their partners, lovers, friends, and family members, particularly their parents. Although it is not always the case, most adults with disabilities appreciated their parents' advocacy on their behalf when they were younger. Later in life, as Liz taught me, not so much. Finally, the disability movement includes professional allies such as teachers, therapists, doctors, and service providers as well as champions from government and business.

This book focuses on five powerful disability advantages.

The Power of Majority

One in seven individuals worldwide has a disability. At 1.2 billion, that makes them the largest minority group on the planet. That's the population of China and almost four times the population of North America. Another three in seven are their families, friends, and supporters. In total, four in seven people in the world have a connection to disability. That's a potent majority. Those kinds of numbers translate into an audience, a base, and a market that's too large to ignore and just waiting to be mobilized, especially since it represents $8 trillion in annual disposable income.[1] By comparison, the much-sought-after teen market is relatively small at $220 billion.[2]

The Power of Inclusivity

The disability movement intersects with every gender, race, ethnicity, color, creed, class, sexual orientation, income level, health condition, living arrangement, and age group. This predisposes people in the disability world to understand difference as a natural fact of life to be welcomed and celebrated, not curtailed or cured. This sensitivity enlarges and enlightens. It encourages us to focus on a person's contributions rather than his or her condition, limitation, or identity.

The Power of Ingenuity

There is no group in history with more consistent experience at making their mark, despite the deck being stacked against them, than people with disabilities. People with disabilities wake up every day to a world not designed for them. They are constantly inventing themselves out of adverse circumstances. They are the original hackers. Many of the innovations we take for granted were solutions to challenges they faced that went on to benefit the wider population. The bicycle, the typewriter, and curb cuts are three examples. There is nothing like a dash of disability to increase your ingenuity and resilience, and to help you deal with the inevitable hiccups and setbacks that accompany everyone's life.

ॐ The Power of Authenticity

Our culture is inexhaustible in its capacity to ignore our reliance on others. It promotes the myth of individualism, independence, invincibility. Problems are sanitized, simplified, and easily resolved if we just have the right attitude or if we find the right savior. More and more of us are rejecting that view of the world. We want hope that is qualified by authenticity, and we are looking for stories that we can relate to. The fact is that more and more people are struggling to get by or are worried about the future, and we expect to see that reality reflected in our leadership, media, stories, and social movements. The disability movement offers a refreshing alternative to the lone hero, usually a man, overcoming overwhelming odds. It reminds us that justice emerges from the bottom up, not the top down, and always in the company of so-called ordinary people who disrupt the status quo in big and small ways.

ॐ The Power of Unity

The ultimate power of disability is as a unifying force. We live in tumultuous times, with the world increasingly fractured and polarized. People want to know they are not alone, that they can be part of something bigger than themselves. The disability community has the power to bridge our divides and bring us together. After all, disability is the world's most common condition. It encompasses diversity, exudes ingenuity and authenticity, and is in the majority! That's an unrivaled combination and force for change.

• • •

I've written this book for three reasons. First, I want to change the popular story about disability because too much of it remains shrouded in myth and misunderstanding. I want to do that by correcting what history and media have overlooked and by giving credit where credit is due.

Second, I want to connect the dots and introduce you to a culture as rich as any religion, philosophy, or self-help movement. Actually, I want to connect the polka dots. I do that to honor Japanese artist Yayoi Kusama, who is known as the "priestess of polka dots." She is considered the most popular artist in the world today, based on gallery and museum attendance, although she was ignored for decades.[3] During the 1960s, she was part of New York's avant-garde art scene and became friends with Andy Warhol. Georgia O'Keeffe was her business adviser. In the early seventies, she returned to Tokyo and became a voluntary patient in a Tokyo psychiatric institution to help her deal with the obsessional images that have pursued her since childhood. She still lives there. I don't want to romanticize the challenges that Kusama had to deal with in order to return to megastar prominence. I do want to validate her experience and to learn from her and many others who have been touched directly or indirectly by disability.

Third, I'd like this book to contribute to the grand awakening that is underway within the disability movement. In my last book, *Impact: Six Patterns to Spread Your Social Innovation*, I concluded that for social change to have lasting impact, it's important to link everyone's actions, big and small, and to get as many people moving in the same direction as possible. People with disabilities shouldn't have to carry the full weight of removing the barriers to their full participation in society—barriers like poverty, inaccessible buildings, inadequate health care, and job discrimination. No amount of positive thinking by individuals will fix those big problems. They are do-it-together, not do-it-yourself, projects.

• • •

The following pages will introduce you to funny, talented, loving, wise, inventive, and artistic people—proof that human ability knows no boundaries when the boundaries are removed and the opportunities to make a difference are available. Like the rest of us, they haven't figured everything out, although the bits they have figured out are impressive. Otherwise, their lives are as messy and full of doubts, failures, and contradictions as those of the rest of us.

Some are lucky in love, some aren't. They worry about getting a job, what will happen to their kids, what people think about them, and lots of other big and little things. Their opinions differ on what to do about climate change, the economy, divisive politics, and a host of other matters. Some vote one way. Some vote another. Some don't vote at all.

You will recognize many of the celebrities and personalities who are profiled in this book, although you may not be familiar with the parts of their lives that I will share, perhaps even their connection to the world of disability. They include Michael J. Fox, Helen Keller, Stephen Hawking, Temple Grandin, Abraham Lincoln, Stevie Wonder, and the Swedish schoolgirl Greta Thunberg. As I was finishing this book, Thunberg had just made the cover of *Time* magazine for encouraging students around the world to go on strike to raise awareness about our climate crisis.[4] On the other hand, you may not know about the relationship between singer Joni Mitchell and jazz legend Charles Mingus after he was diagnosed with ALS. Or about the influence of author Bonnie Klein on her daughter Naomi Klein's activism. Or about rocker Neil Young's lifelong and multiple experiences with disability. Or the reason Anna Sewell wrote *Black Beauty*. Or why Richard Branson, the founder of the Virgin Group, has joined forces with Caroline Casey, the first woman from the West to ride an elephant across India by herself.

I will also introduce you to people you will want to know more about. People like classical musician Evelyn Glennie, who is the world's first full-time solo percussionist. Glennie is deaf, plays in her bare feet in order to "hear," and is on a mission to teach the world how to listen. Then there is Chinese poet Yu Xiuhua, who is considered the Emily Dickinson of China. Her poem "Crossing Half of China to Sleep with You" has been read by millions and has made her the voice of feminism in her country. And Jean Vanier, who gave up a life of privilege to launch a worldwide movement of compassion. He is hailed as one of the world's greatest "spiritual entrepreneurs," in the same company as Billy Graham, Mother Teresa, and the Dalai Lama. And Alice Wong, the writer and media maker who is reinventing activism for the twenty-first century. And Robert Munsch, who wrote Oprah's favorite children's story, "Love You Forever." And Pearl S. Buck, the first American woman to win the Nobel Prize and who changed the course of history by writing openly about her daughter Carol, who had a disability, and why she defied the advice of doctors to place her in an institution and forget about her. I will also profile several people who can spice up your love life.

Whether or not their stories and experiences are recognizable, you will have no trouble relating to them and applying their insights to your everyday life and work.

There are many ways to receive an education in the world. The experience of disability is definitely one of them. *The Power of Disability* distills that wisdom into ten lessons. The lessons blend, overlap, and reinforce each other, as all good lessons do. I didn't invent these lessons. They emerged from what I observed over four decades of activism in the disability movement.

As for Liz, she continues to write and perform poetry, teach art, paint, and offer her work to the public at http://lizetmanski.com. She's also in demand as a graphic recorder, whereby she captures the proceedings of meetings and conferences by drawing on big sheets of paper fastened to the wall. Recently she landed a small role in a new Apple TV series. Her force of character has been strong enough for her to eject herself from my orbit and attract a network of family members, friends, and supporters into her own. She continues to grow in confidence. Sometimes I think I can see it expanding right in front of me. She thinks Down syndrome is "so radiant." It is both no big deal and the real deal to her. I have learned that there is a big difference between sameness and acceptance. It's pretty clear that Liz never did need fixing. Her difference simply needed a home.

Perhaps that's the power and meaning behind Yayoi Kusama's obsession with polka dots. Polka dots are like people, she says: They can't stay alone. It's in their nature to come together, and to find their place in the universe.

May the following pages help you find yours.

A Word about Words

Special needs, differently abled, handicap, or disability?

Mental, intellectual, cognitive or developmental disability?

*Autistic, Asperger's syndrome, autist, high functioning,
autism spectrum disorder (ASD), or neuro-diverse?*

Hearing-impaired, deaf, or Deaf?

*Paralyzed, spinal cord injury, paraplegic, quadriplegic,
wheelchair user, or wheelchair rider?*

Blind, visually impaired, or nonvisual learner?

Mentally ill, mad, or crazy?

WHAT'S CORRECT? WHAT'S OFFENSIVE? In most cases, it depends on context and personal preference. The nomenclature of disability is evolving with the times. It comes complete with its own language, definitions, jargon, and symbols. Although not as complicated as insider baseball, these are under constant renovation, swirling with adjustment, while leaving artifacts and descriptors from the past clinging to life. For example, words like *idiot, imbecile,* and *moron* are still in use. And they are still hurtful.

That's why it is never acceptable to use the word *retarded*, not even in jest. Or to describe someone as "confined" or "bound" to a wheelchair. It's the exact opposite. Wheelchairs, canes, scooters, and other mobility devices represent freedom, liberation, participation. Nowadays Asperger's syndrome is dropping out of use because Asperger was a doctor associated with the Nazis.

A disability includes conditions that have a long-term impact on your mobility, dexterity, seeing, hearing, intellectual development, mental health, or some combination of them. These conditions may affect how you bathe, dress, move around, and interact and communicate with others, as well as how you learn, remember, and concentrate.[1] A disability is not a sickness. There is nothing wrong with the person. It isn't a bad thing. People don't suffer from their disability. If they experience pain or other side effects, those can usually be addressed in the same way you treat and manage yours. Generally, people with disabilities aren't looking for a cure, although I know people who would take a cure if it were available—for example, for a spinal cord injury or Parkinson's disease. At the same time, they are not waiting for a miracle, and they have active, fulfilling lives.

Some disabilities are visible. Most aren't. For example, more than 130 million Americans live with invisible and pain-related disabilities such as brain injury, fibromyalgia, Lyme disease, scoliosis, Crohn's disease, and lupus. You can be born with a disability or acquire one during your lifetime. If you live long enough, you likely will.

All disabilities are accompanied by visible and invisible barriers. These include narrow doorways. Stairs without ramps. Street curbs without cuts. Traffic lights without beeps. Gatherings without sign language interpreters. Language that is complicated, full of big words, and hard to follow. Teachers and institutions that ignore your learning style. And websites that don't use alt text. Alt text is a written description of pictures and images on a website. It tells people who are unable to see and who are using a screen reader the nature and content of the visuals on the web page. Alt text is the equivalent of a wheelchair ramp making the web accessible for many people with disabilities. Some barriers are cultural, as in those beliefs, stereotypes, and attitudes that lead to discrimination, low expectations, and exclusion from the job market, and from society. One of the biggest cultural barriers is poverty. Governments are more willing to allocate money for programs run by professionals than they are to provide individuals with a decent income or give them financial control over the services they use. This reveals a mind-set that people with disabilities don't know or can't be trusted to spend the money on their best interests.

Person First versus Identity First

For decades, most people preferred to be described as a person with a disability. They didn't want to be defined by their disability. That's certainly the way I was schooled. Besides, a diagnosis, category, or label doesn't reveal very much about a person. Certainly not his or her spirit, personality, and character.

There is a new wave of people who prefer to be described as disabled first. The following tweet from a leading disability activist reflects this preference: "I am unapologetically disabled. My choice. My experience. My identity."[2] Disability is central to their lives, and they don't want it pushed into the background. They want to celebrate their disability. This pride in identity has existed for a long time in the deaf community. If you are deaf and identify with Deaf culture, you use a capital *D*. Otherwise, you use the lowercase, *d* as in *deaf*.

Regardless of preference, people with disabilities don't want people who don't have a disability to define who they are. They interpret phrases such as *differently abled, handi-capable, diverseability*, and *special needs* as denying an essential aspect of their identity, and as suggesting that there must be something negative or bad about their disability if people are trying to obscure it.

Some folks are taking back terms like *crip* and *mad*, flipping their negative connotations and breathing positive life into them. The hip-hop community does that too. The word *ill* means "very cool" in their community, which may be one of the reasons why some of hip-hop's biggest stars have a disability. Others poke serious fun at society's fascination with classifications. The Institute for the Study of the Neurologically Typical parodies the idea of normal. They describe normal as "a neurobiological disorder characterized by preoccupation with social concerns, delusions of superiority, and obsession with conformity."[3]

I'll use person-first language (i.e., *a person who has a disability*, as opposed to *a disabled person*) throughout this book most of the time. That decision is based on the recommendations of my friends and colleagues with disabilities whom I consulted. However, should the person I profile have another preference, I will use it. Despite my best efforts, there are bound to be inconsistencies and mistakes, which I apologize for in advance.

As a general rule, if you are wondering what language to use, ask. Don't assume. It could be the start of a beautiful relationship.

If It Ain't Broke, Don't Fix It

Perfection simply doesn't exist. Without imperfection, neither you nor I would exist.
—DR. STEPHEN HAWKING

The culture is constantly telling me, "This kind of body is right and your kind of body is not." So even though I know myself as a whole person, I still daily experience the sense that this is not the right way to be.
—JUDITH SNOW

Parents get so worried about the deficits that they don't build up the strengths.
—TEMPLE GRANDIN

℀ What Gord Walker Taught Me

WE ARE ALREADY as close to perfect as heaven will allow and don't need fixes and cures to make us whole.

The first time I met Gord Walker, he took one look at me and walked out of the room. He had been a client of the disability service system for years, and he could smell a social worker like me from a distance. Gord didn't need any more reminders that social service workers thought he was worthless. I once saw a thick file listing all the programs and interventions he had received since he was a youngster. It included behavior management programs, time-out protocols, one-to-one workers, communication strategies, psychological counseling, and medication. Apparently these weren't working very well, because the file was also full of recommendations to fund more programs and more specialists.

Fortunately Gord gave me and PLAN, the organization I had co-founded, a second chance—a chance to develop a network of friends with him. We recruited a young woman who ignored the diagnoses and assessments that were in Gord's files. She described them as self-fulfilling prophecies. She believed that everyone had a gift, and her job was to help people discover it. She was infused with the spirit of abundance. She was also patient. She sat in silence with Gord for many hours. She didn't offer suggestions. She expected that his dreams would eventually surface.

One day, she came to our office ecstatic. "I've got it," she said. "It's horses." It turned out that Gord loved everything about horses—grooming them, exercising them, cleaning their stalls, and riding them. He even wanted to own one. More than anything, he dreamed of being a cowboy, herding cattle. His passion eventually led to a job at the local stables, where he became affectionately known as the horse whisperer. He attracted a stable of friends too, connected by their shared interest in all things horsey. One of his friends was able to arrange an annual summer job for Gord riding the range as part of the largest cattle drive in southern British Columbia.[1] It was the highlight of his year. He talked about it all the time. "You should come," he would say to me. "There's a campfire party every night."

We live in an age that promises a cure for just about everything. Advertisers sell us products that they claim will make us thinner, faster, and more beautiful. Motivational speakers and personal coaches promise that they can make us or our children smarter, better, richer, and happier. Researchers and better-living advocates promote perfect health: just eat these foods, choose this procedure, take this pill, and practice mindfulness. We are offered a life that would have been unimaginable decades ago. Some technologists, philosophers, and genetic engineers even tantalize us with the possibility that soon all diseases will be eradicated and we can live forever.

The pursuit of perfection has its downsides. We know deep down that a lot of the claims can't be true because, like Gord, we've been disappointed before. Still, the choices keep coming, and they are bewildering. It's not easy to sort out the valuable from the worthless. To top it off, we may start believing that there is indeed something wrong with us and that perhaps we need fixing. Some of us have a deeper unease. The great religions of the world warn us against thinking we can become godlike. Popular culture is full of stories about the downside of selling one's soul to the devil for worldly benefits. It's called a Faustian bargain.

In reality, all of us are a mixture of frailties, inadequacies, mistakes, imperfections, and flaws—as well as a mixture of talents, strengths, and abilities. Accepting that we are all of the above is what makes us whole. The people profiled in this lesson pursue wholeness, not perfection. One believes that imperfection holds the key to the universe. Others understand that healing is different from curing. They have learned to distinguish between "fixing" that is helpful and "fixing" that is hurtful.

My wish is that we wriggle free of the grasp of the needs makers (i.e., advertisers and social service workers who create needs that they then claim they can fix) and recognize that perfection is an illusion that needs to be broken. Most of the time we don't need to be fixed. We need to be listened to and valued.

✃ Body Politics CATHERINE FRAZEE

What needs fixing are the limitations imposed by
society on our ability to belong, love, and contribute.

As a child, Catherine Frazee, poet, activist, and former chief commissioner of the Ontario, Canada, Human Rights Commission, had only one wish: "to be able to walk." Four decades later, in her essay "Body Politics," she asked herself whether she would still make the same wish.[2] The following are excerpts from her essay, written in 2000. It begins with Frazee's two descriptions of her disability:

> In the not so flattering language of medical textbooks, I am a
> flaccid paralytic, suffering from a genetic mutation that causes
> profound and progressive wasting of the skeletal muscles. My
> body has the consistency of overcooked pasta. . . . My body
> does not speak in sentences laid end-to-end and stacked in
> sturdy paragraphs. My not-so-normal body speaks in poetry,
> not prose—in sparing words, in careful disarray.

She acknowledges that many people with disabilities like hers wish
to walk. She mentions that *Superman* star Christopher Reeves "made it
his life's work to walk again." For others, including herself, the seduc-
tions of medical science raise personal, political, and ethical questions.

> The simple arithmetic of it is that my disability has brought
> me smartly to all the things I value—my career, my skills, my
> tenacity, my intimate partner, my world view. And there is no
> logical reason to believe that this will not continue to be the
> case for as long as I remain alive.
>   This is not a matter of simple acceptance, of stoicism, of
> bravely making the best of my sorry lot. It is a matter of growing
> into and embracing my experience of disability. That is not to
> say that I embrace the exclusion, the stigma, the devalued status,
> the abuse, and the barriers that are the constant companions of
> disability. . . . These do not build character. They are as destruc-
> tive and senseless as war is. I feel as impassioned about resisting
> these forces as others must feel about their battles to "find a
> cure." But let me be very clear: stigma, barriers, and exclusion
> are the enemy—not my disability.

A Masai warrior she encountered while on safari in Kenya helped
her understand walking as a way of belonging, of being present and
proud.

> From this Masai warrior, who spoke to me not in words but
> in footsteps, I began to understand the true nature of walking.

To walk as a Masai warrior is to belong—flesh, bone, and soul. It is to declare one's title. It is integral and devout. To walk as a Masai warrior is to assume one's place in the cosmos—no more, and no less.

This, I can aspire to. Perhaps this is what we all wish for, in which case the contributions of medicine and technology will be at best peripheral and at worst impediments. For the purpose of locomotion, I am content to use the fingers of my right hand, the drive-stick of my wheelchair, the wheel, and the electromagnetic miracles that link the latter two so very cleverly together. For the purposes of expression, however, I want to walk as the Masai warrior. Just exactly as I do, when I am present and erect, confident of who I am and where I am going. When I know that I have every right to be here.

⚭ Brilliant Imperfection ELI CLARE

Bodily differences are neither good nor bad.
We are all perfectly imperfect.

Poet, writer, activist, and teacher Eli Clare says that curing his cerebral palsy would completely change who he is.[3] "On an individual level, my cerebral palsy is defined as 'trouble,' both medically and culturally," he said in an interview. "And yet, I don't have any idea who I'd be without tremoring hands, slurring speech, tight muscles, and a rattling walk."[4]

Clare isn't against cures in principle. He makes a distinction between medical cures that save lives, reduce suffering, and prevent diseases, versus eradicating "perfectly imperfect" differences. The culprit is a cure mind-set that is embedded in popular culture. Thus we have weight-loss surgery, facial hair removal, Botox, teeth whitening, skin-lightening creams, and antidepressants, he said.[5]

Clare goes right to the heart of the matter in his latest book, *Brilliant Imperfection: Grappling With Cure.*[6] He says the search for perfection is frustrating, elusive, and dangerous, for everyone. He offers the idea of *giftedness* as an alternative. *Giftedness* means making the best with the knowledge, skills, and abilities you have. It doesn't mean rejecting medical intervention when necessary. It does mean resisting the medicalization of identity. Professionals are always wanting to do something about his tremor, he says, when he all he wants is help for the tension that causes him chronic pain. Bodily differences are neither good nor bad, he says—just a simple fact of life. While acknowledging that there are those who want a cure and who want to reshape their bodies, he says the fact is that disability is more an issue of social justice than a medical condition. The cure mind-set "ignores the reality that many of us aren't looking for cures but for civil rights," he says, so that we live in a world where we assist each other.[7]

In the end, Clare wants "a politics that will help all of us come home to our bodies."[8]

ೞ The Gift JUDITH SNOW

Everyone has a gift, including what others describe as a deficiency or disadvantage. Understanding that may one day save the human race.

Judith Snow was known as the Julia Roberts of the disability community even though she had a love-hate relationship with the word *disability*. "There is no such thing as disability," she declared to audiences.[9] She would invite them to reinterpret her wheelchair and the functional limitations associated with her disability. Her magnetic personality and penetrating intellect attracted loyal followers from around the world. Her objection to the D-word arose from the belief that everyone has a gift, including and especially what others saw as a deficit or a disadvantage. She described a gift as anything that creates a meaningful interaction with at least one other person.

She illustrated her meaning with a story from her high school years.[10] A fellow student was a champion diver with the potential to become an Olympic medalist. The school and surrounding community went out of their way to nurture this young woman's gift. They rearranged her classes, postponed her exams, and provided extra tutoring and coaching. Nothing was too daunting, too costly, or too inconvenient. Everyone wanted to play a part in the young diver's success. They felt fulfilled. Some even got paid jobs out of it.

Snow, by contrast, had trouble even getting into the school building. There was no ramp, and there were no plans to build one. No extra tutoring. No accommodation. Those tasks were left to her parents, even though nurturing Judith's scholarly abilities would have created similar opportunities for fulfillment and meaningful employment. Hurtling yourself headfirst into a swimming pool was a rare talent that happened to be valued, said Snow, whereas the fact that she could move only her thumb and the side of her mouth wasn't, even though it had the same potential to nurture trust and bring meaning to the lives of others—more so, according to Snow's fans.

Snow would often quote in her speeches the prophet Isaiah's caution that if we do not welcome the gifts of strangers, society is doomed to slowly crumble. "I am both disabled and not disabled at the same time," she said. "The question is, from which stance can I live my life most powerfully, both for myself and for the community? From which position am I more able to contribute? More able to experience a fulfilled life?"[11]

✃ A Brief History of Imperfection

DR. STEPHEN HAWKING

Staying curious, being nonjudgmental and open to changing your mind, is the true source of knowledge.

The theoretical physicist Stephen Hawking thrived on his failures, joked about his mistakes, and based his scientific theories on imperfection. "Next time someone complains that you have made a mistake, tell him that may be a good thing," he said.[12] He understood that failure and being wrong are just as important as scientific breakthroughs, psychological insight, or intellectual truth. It didn't seem to matter whether he was right or wrong; both helped get him nearer and nearer to an understanding of the order of the universe. Hawking's healthy skepticism, as well as his sense of humor about his discoveries and theories, got him into trouble with some of his colleagues. They believed that their particular scientific discovery was the end of the matter. They took exception to any suggestion that they could be wrong.

Hawking was twenty-two when he was diagnosed with ALS (amyotrophic lateral sclerosis), a neurological condition that reduced his ability to control his muscles, including those he used for breathing. He was given a few years to live at the time. Instead, he lived another fifty years uncovering scientific secrets of the universe—discoveries he attributed to his disability. "My disabilities have not been a significant handicap in my field. . . . Indeed, they have helped me in a way by shielding me from lecturing and administrative work that I would otherwise have been involved in," he wrote in an article about people with disabilities and science.[13] His book *A Brief History of Time* became an international best seller because he used nontechnical language to describe his insights into what makes the universe tick. It was translated into more than thirty-five languages. When asked how he would design the universe differently, he replied, "If I had designed it differently, it wouldn't have produced me. So that is a meaningless question. I'm prepared to make do with the universe we have, and try to find out what it is like."[14]

Hawking turned being wrong and changing one's mind from a weakness to a strength. He realized that no matter how much we know and how much we analyze and theorize, there are always more dark corners and black holes to expose to the light. "Remember to look up at the stars and not down at your feet," he wrote. "Try to make sense of what you see, and wonder about what makes the universe exist. Be curious."[15]

✿ If It Ain't Broke, Don't Fix It
THE SCHAPPELL TWINS

Not everyone wants to get on the medical treatment train.

The Schappell twins couldn't be more different:

Lori is outgoing. Dori is an introvert.

Lori is street-smart. Dori is book smart.

Lori worked in a laundry room; Dori was a country singer. She won an L.A. Music Award for Best New Country Artist in the 1990s. Her stage name was Reba, after her favorite singer, Reba McEntire.

Lori is able-bodied. Dori has spina bifida.

Lori drinks. Dori is a teetotaler.

Lori likes to spend money. Dori saves it—which is why Lori had to pay to get to see "Reba" perform.

There are a couple of things they agree on:

One is that they hate the rhyming names their parents gave them. So Dori, who identifies as a man, changed her name to George.

The other is that being a conjoined twin does not run their world. They are joined at the forehead but face in different directions. George has a specially designed chair, which is like a barstool on wheels. It's just the right height for Lori to move him around; otherwise, she has to carry him. They believe their lives are less complicated than those of most people. They live in a two-bedroom flat and alternate the nights they sleep in each other's rooms. When Lori goes on dates, George brings a book to read. Because they don't face each other, he can ignore his sister's kissing. "I don't see why being a conjoined twin should stop me having a love life and feeling like a woman," Lori said in an interview.[16]

George knew from a young age that he should have been a boy. "It was so tough, but I was getting older and I simply didn't want to live a lie. I knew I had to live my life the way I wanted."[17] In response, Lori said, "Obviously it was a shock when Dori changed to George, but I am so proud of him. It was a huge decision but we have overcome so much in our lives and together we are such a strong team. Nothing can break that."[18]

The twins have been the subject of numerous profiles. In one, the interviewer asked whether they would choose to be separated if the operation could be done safely. "Why would you want to do that?" replied George. "For all the money in China, why? You'd be ruining two lives in the process."[19]

And when Lori was asked the same question in a documentary, her response was "No."

"Why?" asked the interviewer.

"If it ain't broke, don't fix it," she replied.[20]

❧ Hidden Wholeness PARKER PALMER

Embracing our imperfections makes us whole.
Chasing perfection keeps us from becoming whole.

Parker J. Palmer is an acclaimed author of ten books on education, leadership, spirituality, courage, and social change. He has received thirteen honorary doctorates. He is considered one of the world's leading visionaries.[21] Yet he regards his greatest accomplishment to be surviving three serious bouts with clinical depression, two in his forties and one in his sixties. "Nothing I've ever done has required more fortitude and persistence than surviving that assault on my selfhood and sense of meaning and purpose in life," he said in an interview.[22]

During those periods, Palmer spent months cowering in the darkness and had periods when he couldn't feel anything at all, when it seemed his ego had been shattered. He knows he is not alone, and he is willing to write about it because depression is still a taboo subject. It has been estimated that one in ten Americans experiences clinical depression at some point in their lives.

Palmer considers himself a wounded healer. "I was born baffled and have trusted my bafflement more than my certainties," he said in an interview.[23] He knows everyone is a mixed bag. He believes the most important words he can offer to anyone who is suffering are "Welcome to the human race! Now you enter the company of those who have experienced some of the deepest things a human being can experience."[24]

Palmer founded the Center for Courage & Renewal to close the gap between people's personal and professional lives, and to help them integrate their inner and outer selves. He describes this in his book *A Hidden Wholeness* as a move toward wholeness. "Wholeness does not mean perfection," he cautions, "it means embracing brokenness as an integral part of life."[25] For most people it is a hidden or forgotten wholeness. We compare ourselves with society's image of perfection and find ourselves wanting. Instead, Palmer advises that we "put our arms lovingly around everything we've shown ourselves to be: self-serving and generous, spiteful and compassionate, cowardly and courageous, treacherous and trustworthy." The only way to become whole is to say, "I am *all* of the above."[26] Perhaps this is the true meaning of integration.

Palmer's mental illness taught him that there are no shortcuts to wholeness. It involves waiting, watching, listening, suffering, and honoring small signs of progress. "You work your way through that darkness, or it works its way through you."[27] It's not easy to experience, and it's not easy to watch someone else going through it, either. He suggests being present for another person's pain without trying to fix it, and standing respectfully at the edge of his or her mystery—and misery.[28]

"When people ask me how it felt to emerge from depression," he wrote in his book *Let Your Life Speak*, "I can give only one answer: I felt at home in my own skin, and at home on the face of the earth, for the first time."[29]

⚭ Humanity Passport

NAOKI HIGASHIDA WITH DAVID MITCHELL

Citizenship is a given and shouldn't be based on what others consider normal.

Naoki Higashida wrote the Japanese best seller *The Reason I Jump* when he was thirteen. It has since been translated into thirty-four languages. It features his candid answers to fifty-eight questions about his autism. "Why don't you make eye contact when you are talking?" "Why do you make a huge fuss over tiny mistakes?" And of course, "What's the reason you jump?"

Higashida has now written twenty books, and he is not yet thirty. He doesn't speak; he dictates his books by pointing to characters on a cardboard keyboard. A transcriber types them up. Videos of his creative process are available on YouTube. Talking is troublesome for Higashida. His mind goes blank whenever he tries to speak. "Spoken language is like a blue sea," he wrote. "Everyone else is swimming, diving and frolicking freely, while I'm alone, stuck in a tiny boat, swayed from side to side."[30] However, when he's working on his alphabet grid, he feels as if someone has cast a magic spell and turned him into a dolphin.

David Mitchell, the writer of the best seller *Cloud Atlas*, was so impressed with *The Reason I Jump* that he and his wife, Keiko Yoshida, translated it and Higashida's follow-up book, *Fall Down 7 Times Get Up 8*, into English. He said in an interview that the books helped him understand his own son's behavior. "For the first time I had answers, not just theories. What I read helped me become a more enlightened, useful, prouder and happier dad," he said.[31] In another interview, Mitchell admitted that he didn't have the imagination to afford his son "full card-carrying rights as a human being" until he read Higashida's books. He said that Higashida's writings are a "humanity passport" for people with autism because they challenge the myth that people with autism don't have emotions, imagination, or dreams.[32]

Higashida said in an interview that it would be so much easier if the behavior of people with autism were regarded as another personality type. "What your child needs right now is to see your smile. Create lots of happy memories together. When we know we are loved, the courage we need to resist depression and sadness wells up from inside us."[33] On the other hand, he thinks neurotypical people agonize too much over being left out of the group, and that causes unnecessary conflict in their relationships. "I've learned that every human being, with or without disabilities, needs to strive to do their best, and by striving for happiness you will arrive at happiness," he wrote in *The Reason I Jump*. "For us, you see, having autism is normal—so we can't know for sure what your 'normal' is even like. But so long as we can learn to love ourselves, I'm not sure how much it matters whether we're normal or autistic."[34]

As for the reason he jumps, "When I'm jumping it's as if my feelings are going upward to the sky. Really, my urge to be swallowed up by the sky is enough to make my heart quiver. When I'm jumping, I can feel my body parts really well, too—my bounding legs and my clapping hands—and that makes me feel so, so good."[35]

ᔥ A Culture with No Boundaries

CAREY, SHELLY, AND ZOE ELVERUM

Societal expectations change what's wrong into what's awesome.

When Carey and Shelly Elverum's three-month-old daughter, Zoe, was diagnosed with dwarfism, they were in Edmonton, Alberta, Canada. The medical specialists told them that "something went wrong." When they returned home to Pond Inlet near the Arctic Circle, the reaction from the Inuit people who live there was "Hurray! That's awesome."[36] Inuit elders considered Zoe a special being who should be raised by elders. Teenage girls wanted a baby like her. "Everywhere she was just treated as this wonderful being who had sprung into the middle of Pond Inlet," said Shelly in an interview.[37]

Today Zoe is a typical teenager. She loves *Star Wars* and the color black. Her favorite Taylor Swift line is "If you are lucky enough to be different, don't ever change." She considers herself a NERD (Not Even Remotely Dorky). She is also student council vice president. "I'm getting more and more like my mom," said Zoe, "speaking my mind and joining committees."[38]

A big part of the whirlwind that is Zoe is due to the fact that she lives where she does, said her mom. "People's perspective on dwarfism here is that she's like concentrated orange juice. She is who she is because she hasn't been diluted. So this whole community treats her as a really special, quality, capable person with something to contribute to the community."[39] As a result, Zoe has grown up with a healthy sense of herself, her mom said laughingly. "I'm like everyone else," said Zoe. "Yeah, I know I'm smaller than everyone, but there are advantages to being smaller. I'm Zoe. To me I'm just me."[40]

Did You Know . . .

One of the earliest representations of disability was the Greek god of fire, Hephaestus. To the Romans he was Vulcan. Accounts vary as to the origin of his physical disability. It occurred either at birth or because his foot was permanently injured after he was thrown off Mount Olympus by his mother, Hera, queen of the gods. The only god who worked, he was a master artisan, talented blacksmith, and sculptor. He designed Hermes' winged helmet, Aphrodite's girdle, and Achilles' shield. He also designed a winged chariot to assist him in moving around, the forerunner of today's wheelchair.

Did You Know . . .

Virginia Hall was an American-born spy who worked for the British in occupied France during World War II. She lost her leg in a shooting accident. The Germans considered "the spy with the wooden leg" to be the most dangerous of all Allied spies. They launched a hunt across France to find and destroy "the limping lady." For her bravery she was made an honorary member of the British Empire. She received the US Army's Distinguished Service Cross, the only one awarded to a civilian woman in World War II.

☙ LESSON 2

Funny Things Happen on the Way to the Future

The scariest person in the world is the person with no sense of humour.
—MICHAEL J. FOX

Comedy is free therapy. And if it's done well, the audience and the comic take turns being the doctor as well as the patient.
—MAYSOON ZAYID

When life gives you a wheelchair, make lemonade. —ZACH ANNER

☙ What David Roche Taught Me

COMEDY IS ABOUT surprise. It makes us laugh. It also makes us think. David Roche didn't fool around. As soon as he stepped onstage, he set us up. He asked us to ask him, "What happened to your face?" Some did, although most of us were hesitant. "I thought you'd never ask," he responded, and quickly explained that his facial disfigurement was the result of his being born with a rare noncancerous tumor on the left side of his face. He described it as a combination of veins gone wild, followed by radiation burns and surgeries. "And you're worried about having a bad hair day," he said. "I'm having a bad face day."

With that, the spell was broken. One of the funniest people I've ever met showed us why he has received standing ovations at the White House, the Kennedy Center, and art festivals around the world. He told us about the Church of 80% Sincerity, which is a church for recovering

31

perfectionists.[1] He said that's about as good as it gets, especially in an election year. Roche also explained male intuition, that out-of-the-blue certainty that lets guys know when it's time for a beer. And he told us about the gang he hangs out with. It includes Frankenstein, Freddy Krueger, Quasimodo, Igor, and Leatherface with his chainsaw.

Roche describes himself as facially different. His comedic romps are also deadly serious. He is tired of Hollywood using people with facial differences to symbolize evil. "There is no cinematic metaphor that is more trite and shallow," he wrote in an essay.[2] He is used to being stared at, and then to have people quickly look away—probably to scan the sky for falling comets, he jokes. He's had people spit in his face. Once someone came up to him and said, "Shut up, you deformed, communist faggot." That's like a three-in-one, he told the attendees at a retreat he used to cohost with my wife and me.[3]

I admit that Roche's drawing attention to his disability made me uncomfortable at the time. He was puncturing my overinflated sensitivity and showing that humor is the most fun you can have while effectively challenging and changing people's attitudes. Roche understands that one of the jobs of the people who are visibly disabled is to carry the fears of others so they can pretend that they are normal. His humorous anecdotes lead us laughing all the way toward the punch line—that the real predators are our own fears and insecurities about being defective, unlovable, and unacceptable.

Humor is the original entertainment. Funny faces, raised eyebrows, and mimicry accompanied our evolution as a species and probably sped up the development of language—at least for those who didn't get the joke and needed an explanation! Aside from being its own reward, laughter is a great relaxer and helps us cope with life's challenges. There is lots of evidence that it releases endorphins, which help us manage pain, relieve symptoms, lower blood pressure, sleep better, and reduce anxiety. Laughing together also fosters trust and builds community.

Humor and people from marginalized groups haven't got on well in the past. They've been on the receiving end of cruel and exploitive jokes, they've been the subject of cheap laughs, and they've been denied a sense of humor, which is another way to rob people of their humanity. Perhaps that's why there are so many comedians from minority groups. They are products of cultures that survived partially because they maintained their sense of humor. Humor allows them to explore taboos and prejudices and make a point without getting people's backs up. They know how to put people at ease and then to wisecrack the door open to more serious topics.

The people I've chosen for this lesson have made careers out of turning clichés on their head. They are not just comedic geniuses; they are experts at defusing tension and using humor to promote acceptance. They teach us the flexible and expanding boundaries of good taste. Many have transformed their anger and bitterness into anecdotes so funny that we don't realize we've been taught a lesson. Some are provocative. Some are tongue-in-cheek. They are all funny and take us to places we've never been before.

My wish is that we always find the funny side of life's absurdities. There is nothing like a good laugh to make us feel better and to put us in a good frame of mind to deal with our predicaments. And if that doesn't work, David Roche says he can always get out the chainsaw.

❧ Funny Things Happen on the Way to the Future MICHAEL J. FOX

Humor helps us sort out the difference
between resignation and acceptance.

Michael J. Fox is America's best-loved Canadian. His role as a lovable young Republican helped make *Family Ties* one of the most popular TV shows in the 1980s. Then he became a teen idol superstar as Marty McFly in *Back to the Future*. From there, the accolades started piling up:

Emmys, Golden Globes, honorary doctorates, a star on the Hollywood Walk of Fame, jamming with the Who and Bruce Springsteen, and an Order of Canada. Not bad for a kid who grew up dreaming of becoming a professional hockey player and who still cheers for the Boston Bruins.

In 1998, Fox revealed that he had been diagnosed with Parkinson's disease. Contrary to predictions at the time, he is still working. In fact, most of his acting nominations have occurred since his diagnosis. *Rolling Stone* magazine described him as the toughest man on television. Fox admits that as a Canadian, he has never met a beer he didn't like. He began drinking heavily after his diagnosis. His wife, Tracy Pollan, issued an ultimatum that led to his recovery. In a 2013 interview, Fox said he doesn't need to drink: "I can slur my speech, lose my balance, and have cognitive lapses, so why would I want to?"[4] He has been sober for more than twenty-one years, telling *Rolling Stone* that his "sobriety is old enough to drink."[5]

Fox's trademark comic timing can no longer be scripted. The symptoms of his Parkinson's are unpredictable, and he doesn't always have control over his movements. He told *Rolling Stone* that he no longer frets and sweats about a scene in advance. Instead, he reacts as things happen and goes with the flow. Fox explained that joking about his Parkinson's does not mean resignation. It means acceptance, so that he can focus on taking care of himself. He practices Pilates, watches his health, and is careful about his diet. His wife Tracy has just co-authored *Mostly Plants,* a cookbook containing 101 flexitarian recipes. His brother-in-law is Michael Pollan who writes popular books about food systems. He is also vigilant about his attitude. "One's dignity may be assaulted, it may be vandalized, it may be cruelly mocked, but it can never be taken away unless it's surrendered," he told the BBC.[6]

This philosophy imbues his three best-selling memoirs, including *A Funny Thing Happened on the Way to the Future.* It is also the basis of the Michael J. Fox Foundation. To date, it has funded $800 million in patient-focused research. "The moment I understood this—that my Parkinson's was the one thing I wasn't going to change—I started looking at the things I could change, like the way research was funded," he told Marlo Thomas in a *HuffPost* interview.[7] Fox is constantly assessing the line between hope and false hope. In an interview with *AARP* magazine, he said, "Hope is informed optimism."[8]

✏ Laughing Matters MAYSOON ZAYID

Humor helps change the story.

Maysoon Zayid is a stand-up, sit-down comedian, actress, and tap dancer. She explains that the reason she shakes isn't because she is drunk but because the doctor who delivered her was. His incompetence deprived her of oxygen, which caused her cerebral palsy. The result is that she can walk, run in high heels, and tap dance, and she shakes all the time. But she can't stand without falling down immediately. "It's exhausting," she says. "I'm like Shakira—Shakira meets Muhammad Ali."[9] One of the highlights of her life was actually performing for "the man who floats like a butterfly and stings like a bee, has Parkinson's, and shakes just like me, Muhammad Ali."[10] Her TED Talk, "I Got 99 Problems . . . Palsy Is Just One," has been viewed more than ten million times and been translated into forty-two languages.

Zayid's nonstop banter and sharp humor have made her one of the most recognizable people with a disability on TV. She is currently developing a television sitcom that will make her the first visibly disabled woman to play a leading role in a TV series. "We are not making history; we are changing the story," she said in an interview.[11] She said she is an advocate, not an activist, because "activists don't shower!"[12] As a Muslim public figure, Zayid attracts threats and trolls. She credits supportive parents and friends for giving her the confidence to deal with them. In 2016, she performed a free show for delegates at the Republican National Convention. "I thought it was going to be a tough crowd, but I got so many hugs and so much love," she said in an interview. "I don't think I swung any votes, but I do think I squashed some bigotry."[13]

Zayid admits that it's not all fun and falafel. She says it's harder to be Muslim in America than it is to be disabled, but it's even harder to be a disabled woman than a Muslim because women with disabilities are three times more likely to be attacked than others, and nobody believes them. She jokes that she would win gold in the Oppression Olympics. "I'm Palestinian, Muslim, I'm female, I'm disabled, and I live in New Jersey."[14] Despite that, Zayid says she knows people can't wait to join the disability club. Admit it, she says, "it's Christmas Eve, you're at the mall, you're driving around in circles looking for parking, and what do you see? Sixteen empty handicapped spaces. 'God, can't I just be a little disabled?'"[15]

✎ If at Birth You Don't Succeed ZACH ANNER

Laughing together builds trust and understanding.

Comedian Zach Anner uses humor to catch people off guard and to bring everyone to the same level. "Laughing at somebody is just another way of dismissing them," he says, "but laughing with somebody is a bridge to understanding."[16] He titled his memoir *If at Birth You Don't Succeed: My Adventures with Disaster and Destiny* because he was born two months early, underweight and underprepared for life. He says he has the sexiest of palsies. To prove it, he outlined "Top 10 Things I Wish People Knew about Cerebral Palsy" on YouTube. Number one: "Just because I'm in a wheelchair doesn't mean you can pet me like a dog, and just because I like to pee outside sometimes doesn't make me a dog, and just because I won the Westminster Dog Show last year doesn't mean . . . OMG, am I a dog?"[17]

Anner's big break came when he submitted an audition video to *Oprah's Search for the Next TV Star*. The video went viral, earning him his own TV show, *Rollin' with Zach*. He converted that into a YouTube channel that has had more than ten million hits. One of the reasons is his series *Workout Wednesday*, which helps people "achieve a body like mine" with the biceps of a Greek god simply by doing "feel-good pushups."[18] After they are done, they can drink one of his milkshakes. He calls it a handi-cappuccino.

Anner was a writer and adviser on the sitcom *Speechless* for three seasons. He liked the fact that the series had characters with disabilities who were complicated, were funny, and acted like jerks. He says he's done a really good job of proving that last point. When the show wasn't renewed, he tweeted that he was feeling pretty proud of all that he'd accomplished as a medium talent. Then he remembered white privilege and felt slightly less proud.[19]

✆ Changing the World One Laugh at a Time NIDHI GOYAL

Comedy deals with the elephant in the room.

"I'm blind—so is love. Get over it," begins Nidhi Goyal, India's first blind, female stand-up comedian, in a TEDx Talk.[20] Comedy is part of her nighttime activism. She says it is a great medium to tell complicated stories. Goyal works as an international advocate for disability rights and gender justice during the day. "Women with disability are so often seen as asexual, and we need to establish that they have a sexuality on par with other women," she said in a UN Women interview.[21] In another interview, she said that she has the numbers, issues, and data, but she has realized that "the best way to get people to listen is through comedy. . . . I only say things people think but are too afraid to talk."[22]

Goyal's routine covers arranged marriages, dating on Tinder, and sex. She has no shortage of material from her personal life. Once she was asked, "How do you come?" while in an aquasize class. At first she thought it was an obscene personal question. Then she realized the question was about how she got to the pool. "I come alone," she said, "I go alone, I travel alone." She told the TEDx audience, "I really wanted to tell her that with the level of sex education Indian men have, most Indian women come alone!"[23] Another time, a man telephoned her to say he wanted her to meet his son. "I told him I'm visually impaired, and he became speech impaired," she said. He started to stammer and stutter. That was when she realized that her disability was contagious, she joked.[24]

After one of Goyal's performances in Calcutta, a woman from the audience came up to her and said she was falling off her seat laughing and cringing at the same time. The woman realized that Goyal was describing her thoughts about people with disabilities. "To do comedy," Goyal said in an interview, "you need to be strong enough to point to that elephant in the room, which everyone is pretending is not there. And that's something I've done since childhood."[25]

✿ Don't Worry, He Won't Get Far on Foot
JOHN CALLAHAN

Cartooning takes people out of the suburbs of their mind.

John Callahan once said he became a cartoonist because he was already sitting down, which was his way of turning the tables on those who think people with disabilities don't have a sense of humor. Callahan, who died in 2010, became paralyzed at the age of twenty-one when the car in which he was a passenger crashed into a telephone pole. Both he and the driver had been on a drinking spree. The driver escaped major injury, something that took Callahan a long time to accept. Cartooning became an outlet for his anger and his quick wit. He credited his black humor for bringing him out of his depression after the accident.

His cartooning style was described as macabre, politically incorrect, and dark. He specialized in turning clichés on their head, pushing buttons, and challenging taboos. Few groups escaped his needling—liberals, conservatives, doctors, lawyers, feminists, the homeless. At the peak of his popularity, his cartoons appeared in more than two hundred newspapers. They occasionally led to boycotts and protests. In response, he created a section on his website for hate mail.

His cartoons targeting people with disabilities were among his most controversial, although not to people with disabilities. "My only compass for whether I've gone too far is the reaction I get from people in wheelchairs, or with hooks for hands," Callahan said. "Like me, they are fed up with people who presume to speak for the disabled. All the pity and patronizing. That's what is truly detestable."[26]

Callahan's memoir *Don't Worry, He Won't Get Far on Foot* was made into a movie of the same name starring Joaquin Phoenix. The title comes from the caption of his cartoon that shows a sheriff's posse surrounding an empty wheelchair in the desert. When the rights to his autobiography were first optioned, he asked that it not be called *Children of a Lesser Quad*, a reference to the movie *Children of a Lesser God*, which starred Marlee Matlin, who is deaf. He may have enjoyed pushing buttons, but he was also deeply religious. He described what he did as survivor humor. "All these things that happened to me in my life, they have deepened life for me," he told a reporter. "I draw things that are real to me. That includes death, poverty, and sickness, as well as love, profit, and religion."[27]

❦ Get Down Moves LAUREN POTTER

Decency knows the difference between
a good joke and a mean-spirited one.

Actress Lauren Potter is best known for making her character Becky Jackson on the TV show *Glee* the most famous cheerleader in history. Becky doesn't have the sweet, lovable personality that people mistakenly associate with Down syndrome. She's feisty and sassy. "You should see my dance moves," says Becky. "My mom says I have Get Down Syndrome."[28] She can be mean and disagreeable too. She schemes with coach Sue Sylvester to destroy the school's glee club. "I'm Queen Bee, and I can sting like a bitch!"[29]

Offscreen, Potter is just as witty and poised. She got her first standing ovation when she was four, and she began dreaming of being an actress. When people told her that would never happen, she replied, "Just watch me."[30] After being appointed to the President's Committee for People with Intellectual Disabilities by President Obama, she said she didn't meet him but did meet the first dog.

Potter knows the difference between a good joke and a mean-spirited one. "I have Down syndrome and human decency," she recently tweeted. "I want to live in a world where everyone can live, go to school, and go to work without having to be afraid," she wrote on HuffPost. "Afraid of being judged, afraid of being bullied or cyber-bullied. Afraid of new things. Afraid of failure. Afraid of dreaming. In fact, I want to live in a world where people are actually celebrated for their differences, just as I celebrate mine!"[31] She is featured in the children's book *Good Night Stories for Rebel Girls, Vol 2*. "I only listened to the people who told me I could," she said in an interview. "Don't ever give up your dreams, no matter how hard it is or how impossible it seems."[32]

✆ Smart Ass Empire MIKE ERVIN

Satire reveals the truth.

Mike Ervin is an author, blogger, playwright, and disability rights activist living in Chicago. He has a rapier-sharp wit and a fondness for the word *cripple*. Ervin has muscular dystrophy and was a poster child for Jerry Lewis's telethon when he was younger. As he got older, he realized that the telethon's primary purpose was to sanctify Lewis while perpetuating pity toward children with disabilities. He founded Jerry's Orphans to protest the telethon. He has used his wheelchair as a podium ever since. He's been arrested more than a dozen times for civil disobedience.

His blog *Smart Ass Cripple* has been "expressing pain through sarcasm since 2010."[33] It is not for the easily offended or humor impaired, he says, because he wants to cause conflict in people's minds. He explained the reasoning behind the title as follows: "Everybody loves a cripple but everybody hates a smart ass. You'll want to love smart ass cripple because I'm a cripple and it's un-American not to love a cripple. But you won't be able to love smart ass cripple because I'm a smart ass, and nobody likes a smart ass."[34]

His friend and fellow Chicagoan, the late film critic Roger Ebert, described Ervin's writing as "some of the fiercest and most useful satire on the web." Ebert said that humor can be "the most effective political weapon" and that Ervin's "[unleashes] a torrent of truth that makes us laugh helplessly because we know it is true."[35] One of Ervin's ideas is "Rent-A-Cripple."[36] It's a service offered to people who have to stand in long lines, especially at Christmas. Rent-A-Cripple matches them with a person who uses a wheelchair. Then they'll be waved to the front of the line. Rent-A-Cripple comes with other advantages, he says: temporary employment for the person with a disability and a boost to your reputation for being associated with someone with "special needs." He warns that it doesn't come with a money-back guarantee.

❧ Funny, You Don't Look Crazy
VICTORIA MAXWELL

Timing is important in comedy and healing.

Victoria Maxwell is a mental health speaker and actor. She uses her talents and sense of humor to educate people about mental illness and to give people a sense of hope that mental illness is treatable and that there are solutions. She describes herself as "the bipolar princess," referring to a condition she was diagnosed with when she was twenty-five. For five years she denied it, hoping it would go away and trying alternative remedies. When she found herself running down the street naked "towards God," she realized that she needed medical help.[37]

The road to recovery included turning her creativity into *Crazy for Life*, a one-person stage show at a disability arts festival. The response was overwhelming. The audience was in the palm of her hand, laughing, loving, and learning along with her. I know because I was there. It kick-started a career performing theatrical keynotes, writing a regular blog for *Psychology Today*, and becoming a self-described wellness warrior. "I laugh when I think of how life works. I would never have the career I do had I not gone crazy in the first place!" she wrote in *Psychology Today*.[38]

In a piece titled "Rules for Making Fun of Mental Illness," she wrote, "There are times when having a mental illness just begs for some levity."[39] She believes that our funny bone is our most effective and economical health tool when used with respect and discretion. Here are short extracts from her three rules, which serve as general guidelines for laughing with someone and not at their expense.[40]

1. Only If You've Been There, Done That
If you've been there, done that—you can joke about it.
If you haven't, you can't. It's that simple.

2. Laugh with Us, Not at Us

I don't want you to make fun of me for being crazy. But I
do want you to laugh with me when I make jokes about it.

3. Timing Is Everything

Laughing prematurely when I've yet to process a painful
event isn't helpful. Cracking a joke before enough time has
passed can make me feel worse.

Did You Know . . .

The parody website Institute for the Study of the Neurologically Typical released a report showing that an estimated 98 percent of the world's banking
leadership, prior to the financial collapse of 2009, were non-autistic. It urged
regulatory bodies to carefully study the impact of an overrepresentation of
non-autistic people in the banking sector. It suggested that "the focus on ab-
stract instruments (really worthless pieces of paper or bits in a computer system,
with no actual strong financial backing) rather than concrete investments (tied
to actual ability to repay) may be a weakness of the non-autistic mind." Equally
frightening, they reported, many of these same leaders are still in a position to
cause financial damage.[41]

Did You Know . . .

Australian comedian Hannah Gadsby says her best work came after she was
diagnosed with autism. That includes her popular Netflix special *Nanette*, which
focuses on gender and sexuality. She says that the success of *Nanette* is partly
due to her ability to see patterns and to not let the world determine how she
should behave.[42]

Label Jars, Not People

℘ What Cradle Heaven Taught Me

WE ARE A society hiding behind labels. They are society's denial machine.

In the 1980s, I was leaked disturbing news. There had been twelve deaths in eighteen months at Cradle Heaven, a small institution for people with severe and complicated disabilities.[1] There had been no inquest into the cause of their deaths and no review of the facility's license. I went to investigate. It was the most overcrowded institution I had ever been in. Despite the facility's name, most of the people who lived there were adults. They had outgrown their cribs but still lay in them, day and night. When I asked the operators why so many had died, they answered, "It's because they are severely disabled. And everyone knows the severely disabled die young."

It was a perverse logic I was to hear from most officials as we pressed for a public investigation. That included government officials who resisted the inquiry for months and the press who attacked us for undermining the reputation of the "poor devoted saints" who ran the facility. Even the doctor who attended to the facility made the same argument. When I offered to debate him, he declined. Perhaps he knew that other doctors were prepared to testify that the designation "severely disabled" was not a predictor of longevity and that others who had equally complex medical conditions were living and thriving in the community. Perhaps he knew the inquiry would reveal that many of the residents of Cradle Heaven had broken bones that had never been treated, never been set. Perhaps he was of the opinion that people with severe disabilities don't feel pain. Such is the destructive power of labels to objectify and depersonalize—and to legitimize abuse, neglect, and worse.

Labels, even when well intentioned or used for humor, are loaded with judgments and assumptions. They are a lazy, short-form way of thinking. They prevent us from seeing the person behind the label. At their most tragic, labels deny personhood, citizenship, love, and life. And they have the power to destroy spirits, undermine confidence, exclude, and abuse.

We all use labels. We label by political and sexual preference, race, religion, gender, personality, looks, body size, status, ideology, age . . . the list goes on. I do it. You do it. Even though we know better and don't like being labeled ourselves. Beneath these labels are society's myths. These myths find their way into our cultural water supply. They float through our playing fields, school hallways, screens, and corridors of power. They seep into our beliefs and become bedrock. That's when we get into big trouble. When a majority of society believes something is morally right, it ignores evidence to the contrary. Facts don't seem to matter. If necessary, they can be adjusted.

The people profiled in this lesson refuse to reduce their complex lives or the lives of others to a simple category, caricature, or sound bite. They are refreshing our language to remove words that confuse and distort. They are throwing out inaccurate myths. Some are flipping stereotypes on their head. One traces the origin of the destructive labels associated with disability to a scientist who falsified data and then struck an unholy alliance with doctors, lawyers, and politicians. This began the eugenics era in the early twentieth century and led to mass sterilization and later genocide. It also produced too many Cradle Heavens.

The idea behind this lesson is that understanding, not judgment, clears up our thinking and our language and changes how we treat each other. My wish is that we make the time to develop our views and values from gentle, respectful face-to-face encounters with people—from the relationship up, rather than from the label down.

✃ The Mismeasure of Man   STEPHEN JAY GOULD

A fabricated scientific research study unleashed
a century of harm toward people with disabilities.

In 1913, a social scientist by the name of Henry Herbert Goddard published *The Kallikak Family: A Study in the Heredity of Feeble-Mindedness*. It became a best seller. It was based on the family tree of Deborah Kallikak, who was living in an asylum for people with developmental disabilities. Goddard described feeblemindedness as a "clog in the wheels of human progress."[2] He created an IQ test dividing so-called feebleminded people into three categories: morons, imbeciles, and idiots. Goddard's book was used by social scientists, doctors, and lawyers to justify mass sterilization of people with developmental disabilities, making it illegal for feebleminded people to marry, and passing "ugliness laws" prohibiting the "unsightly" from being seen on the street. His book played a significant role in spreading the doctrine of eugenics, the belief that some groups are morally and intellectually inferior because of race, class, education, and intelligence.

There was one catch, however. Goddard had lied. He had made up the whole story. His fabrication and deceit extended to doctoring the pictures of Deborah Kallikak to make her look sinister and dark. The true story behind the Kallikak family, scientific racism, and biological determinism was revealed by evolutionary biologist Stephen Jay Gould in his book *The Mismeasure of Man*. In it, Gould exposed the fallacies and bias of IQ (intelligence quotient) testing. "I would rather label the whole enterprise of setting a biological value upon groups for what it is: irrelevant, intellectually unsound, and highly injurious," he wrote.[3]

Goddard concluded his book by stating that sterilization was not likely to be the "final solution." If that phrase is familiar, it is because it is associated with Hitler. The tragic fact is that Hitler used the eugenics arguments of scientists like Goddard to reinforce his and the Nazis' deadly intent, even though by then Goddard had recanted and reversed his opinions. The Nazis began their mass killing experiments by killing people with physical and mental disabilities. By the end of World War II, they had exterminated an estimated three hundred thousand people with disabilities.

"The most erroneous stories are those we think we know best—and therefore never scrutinize or question," wrote Gould in *Full House: The Spread of Excellence from Plato to Darwin*.[4] "People talk about human intelligence as the greatest adaptation in the history of the planet," he said in an interview. "It is an amazing and marvelous thing, but in evolutionary terms, it is as likely to do us in as to help us along."[5] Gould was declared a Living Legend by the US Library of Congress in 2000. Goddard's deceit, on the other hand, ushered in a century of broken hearts, wasted lives, and cruelty.

ஃ The Power of Not Fitting In   TEMPLE GRANDIN

Be careful who you label. They may save the world.

Temple Grandin has been described as "The Woman Who Thinks Like a Cow." *Time* magazine named her one of the world's 100 most influential people for revolutionizing the humane treatment of cattle. Half the livestock in the US and Canada that are sent to a meat plant are in a humane container system that she designed. In 2017, she was inducted into the American Academy of Arts and Sciences for her understanding of the animal mind. "Animals are highly responsive to a person's tone of voice," she wrote in her guide to working with farm animals. "They can tell the voices of people who have treated them gently and with kindness from those who have been abusive or assisted in a painful procedure."[6]

Grandin was not treated gently or kindly when she was young. The only times she was not teased and bullied were when she was with people who shared similar interests, in electronics lab or out riding horses. She was called a tape recorder because she repeated things over and over in a monotone voice. She knew she didn't fit in but didn't understand why. What saved her was a science teacher who encouraged her to tinker. Her father's toolbox was more interesting to her than her mother's jewelry box. "I am what I do rather than what I feel," she said in an interview.[7] She empathizes with quirky, geeky kids and urges kids to put down their video games and tinker.

Grandin wishes people would have a better understanding of the autistic mind, including parents who want their child's condition cured and their behavior modified. She has a no-nonsense way of talking. She says that if we got rid of the genes that cause autism, we would not have people like Nikola Tesla, whom many consider the true father of the electric age because he discovered the electric alternating current

(AC) that powers the world. Without autism, she says, there would be no Mozart or Einstein. Einstein didn't speak until he was three, she says in a video posted on her website. Furthermore, she jokes, we wouldn't have computers or people to fix them. Instead, she says, we'd have a bunch of people standing around in a cave, chatting and socializing and not getting anything done.

To Grandin, some labels are worse than others. "If I could snap my fingers and be non-autistic, I would not," she said in a TED Talk. "Autism is part of who I am." Besides, "being a woman in a man's world is harder than having autism."[8]

⌘ Dethroning Stereotypes PETER DINKLAGE

*Sometimes there is no choice but to wrestle
labels to the ground and bury them.*

Peter Dinklage took the part of Tyrion Lannister on *Game of Thrones* because his character wielded power and had his fair share of sex and other debaucheries. And Tyrion would stop at nothing to advance his interests, including killing his father. That pretty much upends society's dominant characterization of people with disabilities, including those who have dwarfism. Dinklage wasn't interested in playing the stereotypical jolly dwarf with a long beard and pointy toes, which is why he vetoed Tyrion's having a long beard. "Anything that opens up people's perceptions a bit is good," said Dinklage in an interview.[9] "Bad guys are complicated characters. It's always fun to play them. You get away with a lot more. You don't have a heroic code you have to live by," he said in another interview.[10]

Dinklage is one of the highest-paid actors on television, winning a Golden Globe and three primetime Emmys. His character was one of the series' most popular. Its creator, author George R. R. Martin, admits that the producers didn't know what they would have done if Dinklage hadn't accepted the part. Dinklage's dry humor, wit, and personality are in keeping with the character of Lannister. He survived in a world of military might by beating people to the punch and by entertaining them. Many other characters in *Game of Thrones* were power-wielding characters who were also, as Tyrion Lannister described, cripples, bastards, and other broken things. Martin was deliberate about challenging the fear of becoming disabled because "fear cuts deeper than swords."[11]

Dinklage was constantly reminded of his size when he was growing up. He says that dwarves are still the butt of cruel jokes. When he accepted his Best Supporting Actor award at the 2012 Golden Globes, he paid tribute to Martin Henderson. He knew that people wouldn't know Henderson's name, so he asked them to Google it. Henderson was a person with dwarfism from Somerset, England, who was badly injured after being picked up and thrown by a drunken rugby fan in a bar. Henderson has since died. "You'd be surprised at how condescending people can be," Dinklage said in an interview.[12]

❧ Identity Complications CRISTINA HARTMANN

Identity has its advantages and disadvantages.

Cristina Hartmann encountered sound for the first time when she was six. She was one of the first children in America to get a cochlear implant, a bionic ear that enabled her to hear and speak to a certain extent. Cristina Hartmann used sign language to communicate for the first six years of her life because she did not hear. Then she became one of the first children in America to get a cochlear implant, a bionic ear that enabled her to hear and speak to a certain extent. Twenty years later a fog rolled in. She wrote, "my vision took a nosedive and left me legally blind."[13] Today Hartmann is a lawyer turned writer and an explorer—of countries and identities. She describes herself as having faded vision and pixelated hearing—neither quite blind nor quite deaf.

Hartmann has a complicated relationship with her identities. Her parents are Brazilian. She doesn't know Portuguese. She grew up more deaf than Brazilian. Nevertheless, she was teased and ostracized by other deaf students for having a cochlear implant. They rejected implants as suggesting that there was something wrong with them—as an attempt to undermine their natural sign language.

"Where did I belong," Hartmann writes, "amid this constellation of identities: Deaf, hearing, Brazilian, American, blind?"[14] Books saved her. They taught her that she was more than a label. The more she read, particularly about other minority groups, the more she began to understand "that we're all more similar than different."[15]

Reading developed in her a serious case of wanderlust. Her travels reinforced her belief that it's our struggles that unite us. Her pride in her deafness didn't mean she had to close herself off from the wider world. "The Deaf world is a wonderful, bracing place, but it is a small place," she wrote in an essay.[16] "I might've been a heterosexual, light-skinned Latina with a complex Deaf identity, but that didn't mean I couldn't identify with a gay Black boy from the 1940s or an Arab girl in some dystopian future," she wrote in another essay.[17]

Note: Those who are deaf and identify with Deaf culture use a capital *D*, and those who are deaf but don't identify with the culture use the lower case.

✂ The R-Word TIMOTHY SHRIVER

Some words hurt no matter how funny we think they are.

Timothy Shriver inherited a tough political hide. His uncle was President John F. Kennedy. Shriver is used to criticism, including self-criticism. "I used it when I was a kid," he admitted in an interview.[18] He was referring to the word *retarded*, the R-word. "There was no sensitivity to this language. No public consciousness," he added.[19]

Shriver is the current chair of Special Olympics, which involves nearly five million athletes and one million volunteers in 172 countries. While continuing its focus on sports, he wants to eliminate harmful slang about people with developmental disabilities. "It is much bigger than a word, but words matter. And the word 'retard,' whatever its history, reflects a massive problem," he wrote in a *Washington Post* op-ed.[20]

That's why he is backing the Spread the Word to End the R-Word campaign. The campaign encourages people to take a pledge to stop using the word *retard*. In the *Post* op-ed, Shriver wrote, "We are fighting a word because it represents one of the most stubborn and persistent stigmas in history."[21] It's a symbol of a pain that few realize exists, even when it's not directed at people with developmental disabilities. In 2010, Shriver took Rahm Emanuel, then President Obama's chief of staff, to task for using the R-word to describe some of his political opponents. Emanuel subsequently apologized and pledged to stop using the word. "Name-calling is a subtle but malicious practice that only serves to perpetuate stigma, fear, intolerance, and more," Shriver wrote in a CNN commentary.[22]

Note: I use the phrase *developmental disability* instead of intellectual disability because intelligence and consciousness always develop and expand.

❧ Breaking the Silence ALLIE CASHEL

Sharing stories breaks the stigma for people who have invisible disabilities.

Allie Cashel no longer suffers in silence, and she wants to help the other 133 million North Americans who experience chronic, disabling illnesses to do the same. "For a long time I was terrified to tell people about my illness experience because I was scared they wouldn't believe me," said Cashel in an interview.[23] "I needed to become an advocate for myself, especially in conversations about my controversial diagnosis. I had doctors tell me I was having a mental breakdown and needed to find the strength to tell them otherwise," she said.[24] Cashel was diagnosed with Lyme disease when she was seven. During her senior year of high school, she lost her ability to read, struggled to speak, and had major lapses of memory. She left school for three months to recover.

Cashel wrote her book *Suffering the Silence: Chronic Lyme Disease in an Age of Denial* to break the stigma and counter the ignorance associated with chronic diseases. These include brain injury, chronic pain, lupus, being HIV positive, Crohn's disease, endometriosis, diabetes, fibromyalgia, migraines, hemophilia, scoliosis, colitis, and Lyme disease. Lyme has become the first disability associated with climate change. Its prevalence is on the rise in the Northern Hemisphere because warmer temperatures are encouraging the tick that spreads the bacterium to head north.[25]

Cashel also cofounded with Erica Lupinacci the organization Suffering the Silence. They are addressing the misunderstanding, judgment, rejection, and loneliness experienced by people who aren't visibly sick or disabled and whose fatigue and pain are hard to measure. They want people to know they are not alone and work to teach people to become their own advocate. Their website (www.sufferingthesilence .com) is resplendent with beautiful photo essays of those who live with chronic illness. It also offers tips for breaking the silence, such as speaking up on your bad days, asking for help, being honest about your limits, connecting with others who have chronic illness, and letting go of relationships that aren't helping you to heal.

Talking about Lyme disease has been an important part of Cashel's healing. "Once I started owning the truth of my experience with this disease, I found empathy in people and conversations that I never expected to find. Hearing other people share their experiences with illness helped me to better understand my own," she wrote.[26]

✆ Label Jars, Not People EDITH SHEFFER

Labels have long-term negative cultural impact.

Historian Edith Sheffer dedicates her book *Asperger's Children* to her son Eric, who she says suffers from an act of classification. One day when her son was in fourth grade, his teacher showed the class images of various disabilities, including one describing autism. It depicted a boy playing with trains, in his own little world, no eye contact, no interest in others. Her son came home in shock. He slammed the cartoon on the table. "Is this me? Is it really me?" he asked his mom.[27] She said her son was so upset that he wanted to have brain surgery in order to take autism out of his head.

Sheffer's book indicts Asperger as a Nazi sympathizer who sent many of his patients with a disability to their death. Ironically, Asperger's syndrome is a category he never used. She believes that all-encompassing classifications imprison children. It affects their perceptions of themselves as well as how others treat them. "Labels are powerful, with histories and consequences that reach far beyond the individuals who issue them," she wrote.[28] She is pleased that the classification Asperger's syndrome has been removed from the manual that classifies mental conditions.

Sheffer reminds people that hysteria was once a common medical diagnosis for women. Although it is no longer recognized, its negative cultural impact still lingers. "While hysteria was a diagnosis of supposedly overemotional women, autism could be seen as a diagnosis of supposedly under emotional boys," she wrote.[29]

"Labels can be helpful when they're helpful," Sheffer said in an interview. "Right now we are not at a place in the nomenclature where autism is a helpful label."[30] She ends her book with a written statement by her son that reads in part, "People with autism should be treated like everyone else, because if they are not, it will make them be even less social."[31]

✎ Branding Disability ALBERT LASKER

The advertising industry can teach us to
counteract negative stereotypes and images.

Albert Lasker is known as "the man who sold America." He invented modern advertising, creating brands that have survived for a hundred years or more. They include Kleenex; Puffed Wheat and Puffed Rice, the food "shot from guns"; Sunkist oranges; Goodyear's All-Weather Tread; and Sun-Maid raisins. He once took a soap made from palm and olive oil that wasn't selling well. He rebranded it as Palmolive, and it became the best-selling soap in the world at the time.[32]

Lasker saw advertising as a force for social good. While an issue has to stand on its own merits, he believed that advertising could help pull, not push, the general public in the direction of being more supportive. He rebranded the Birth Control Federation as Planned Parenthood because it sounded more constructive and would meet with less opposition. He gave the American Society for the Control of Cancer, which was struggling to generate donations, the name it still has, the American Cancer Society. He felt its name was weak and didn't promote the benefits—i.e., searching for a cure. After the name change, the donations started pouring in.[33]

Lasker had a long association with disability. His first wife, Flora, had a disability, and he lived with depression all his adult life. He took several extended leaves of absence from work. Even after he had become the most powerful advertising man in America and had made an enormous fortune, he still shook with anxiety before meeting a new client.

If he were alive today, I think he would see the association between brands and people with disabilities as a good thing: that they represent moments in the cultural transformation of the disability identity and are a testament to the incalculable number of actions taken by an inconceivable number of advocates in the past. The examples of corporate association with disability are mounting. Mattel has created a Barbie who uses a wheelchair and another who has a removable prosthetic limb.[34] *National Geographic* now promotes accessible travel. It recently devoted two issues of its Polish edition to portraits of people with disabilities.[35] Disability-themed emojis are available on Apple, Google, Microsoft, Samsung, Facebook, and Twitter platforms. And Lucas Warren of Dalton, Georgia, was chosen as 2018's Gerber baby.[36] The reasons are obvious. He is cute as a button, has a magnetic smile and Down syndrome.

Perhaps something is changing for the better in popular culture. Differences are being normalized. It's becoming attractive to be associated with disability.

Did You Know . . .

In 1972, Geraldo Rivera exposed the overcrowding and abuse at the Willowbrook State School. His series *Willowbrook: The Last Great Disgrace* won him a Peabody Award. It is credited with ending the United States' policy of institutionalizing people with developmental handicaps. Rivera considers the subsequent shift to small community-living residences as his most important contribution to society.

Did You Know . . .

Before Alexander Graham Bell invented the telephone, he was a teacher of the deaf. Both his mother and his wife were deaf. He believed in eradicating deafness by promoting lip reading and suppressing the use of sign language. This caused a negative impact on Deaf culture that continues today. It attempted to take away their language and stigmatized a perfectly valid method of communication.

There Ain't No Cure for Love

Even in love, people don't really understand what attracts them to each other. —YU XIUHUA

Because we are told we are not sexy or lovable it becomes a bigger deal than it is. And we start blaming the world and other people.
—MIK SCARLET

The biggest misconception about disability and sex is that people who are disabled don't have sexual desires and probably don't have sexual partners either because they're not desirable. —KALEIGH TRACE

CB What Phil and Wendy Allen Taught Me

THERE IS A wealth of Hollywood-style imagery about sex in our society, yet a poverty of understanding about sexuality, love, and intimacy. People with disabilities can help. They can shine a light in the dark corners of our desire and expand the boundaries of commitment, particularly as we age, become a caregiver to a partner, and experience long-term illness or impotency.

I taught a summer school university course on disabilities for classroom teachers for a number of years. My teaching method was simple: introduce them to as many people with disabilities and their families as possible. The most powerful guests were always Phil and Wendy Allen. I had known them separately before they started courting. Wendy was vivacious and could light up any dance floor. She cohosted a radio show on disability. Phil was older, an authority on John Wayne westerns and

Star Trek. He was one of the few people ever to escape from an institution for people with developmental disabilities. He simply walked away from the place, where, in his words, "the only thing they taught you was how to feel forgotten."[1]

From the moment Phil and Wendy walked into the class, you could feel the sympathy factor heightening. Despite making it clear in my introduction that Phil and Wendy were there to talk about love and commitment, the first questions always focused on their experience of disability. Eventually the penny dropped. The tender way in which Phil and Wendy related to each other made it clear that they were still sweethearts after years of marriage. The class realized that it should have stuck to the topic. The rest of the class resembled a session with Dr. Ruth. It never failed. Many were struggling with their own relationship and used the class to seek advice from the Allens on how to recover from a broken heart, how to share household chores, and how to make love last through bumps and misadventures. The teachers became students.

Phil and Wendy were married at a time when few people with developmental disabilities got married. Most weren't allowed to. Nor were they allowed to have sex, as if that could be prevented. Phil once told me that he had had a girlfriend in the institution, but staff never knew about it because if they were caught, they would each be put in an isolation room. Sex and disability rarely go together in the popular mind-set. Sadly, desire, romance, and reproduction aren't associated with disability either, which is too bad because people with disabilities, as Phil and Wendy taught my classes, can liberate us from the damaging myths associated with love and sexuality.

The people I've chosen for this lesson are incurably romantic. They are also hot and desirable. They think about sex as much as we do—or as little. They likely know every combination of love, lust, and infatuation, and how to extend and reinvent one's sexuality. They have a lot to teach us about the pleasures and joys associated with the laws of attraction.

My wish is that all our relationships be tender ones. That we always consider the body and the soul. And that we remember that it's not how we are made, how we look, or how we are changing and aging that is important. It's how we love, and are loved.

⌘ Hot, Wet, and Shaking KALEIGH TRACE

Confidence is sexy.

Kaleigh Trace used to feel guilty about sex. Not any longer. "I like it. I have it and I never once feel bad about it," she says.[2] Today she feels guilty about other things, like not doing yoga, not knowing how to cook, and eating yogurt for dinner. She describes herself as a disabled, queer, and feminist sex educator who uses words and dildos.

Trace was nine years old when a car accident damaged her spine. She spent her childhood in a wheelchair. Today she uses a cane and describes herself as ambling around with a serious swagger. It took her a long time to learn that a disability may redefine your body but not your sexuality. The lengthy delay was partly because she missed out on sex ed. It was delivered in gym classes, which she didn't attend because she had a disability. She also had to "annihilate a lot of weird guilt feelings about sex"[3]; reject the message that women are supposed to be thin and beautiful receptacles for men; and accept the idea that erotic, pleasurable sex doesn't necessarily mean putting things in things. As a teenager, she became self-conscious about her disability. It's easy to love having blond hair and blue eyes, she told a radio interviewer, but harder to love the parts of her body that were different. "I think I more actively love the parts of my body that aren't normative. I really love my feet, even though they look so different."[4] She has made it her personal project to stop being ashamed of herself.

Her memoir, *Hot, Wet, and Shaking: How I Learned to Talk About Sex*, is about "the things we don't talk about—the mystery, the expectations, and the bullshit that can go along with sex," according to her publisher.[5] During her twenties, she worked in a sex shop, which helped her redefine conceptions of beauty, value, and desirability. "I wish that every single adult knew that they are totally hot and sexy just as they are," she said in an interview. "So many people of all ages and genders tell me they need to lose weight or have a bigger penis or clearer skin in order to have better sex, and I just want to tell each of them that confidence is what is really sexy."[6]

ॐ There Ain't No Cure for Love

LEONARD COHEN

Love is its own drug.

Leonard Cohen thought he had found a cure for the love he sang about in "Ain't No Cure for Love." He thought he had reached some kind of higher plateau where he didn't need sex—until he realized that it was a side effect of the medication he was taking for his depression. "That stuff crushes your libido," he said in an interview.[7] So one day, when he was driving to the airport, he stopped the car and threw the pills out the window. "If I am going to go down, I would rather go down with my eyes wide open," he said.[8] Cohen was known as the troubadour of sadness and the godfather of gloom. "I've dealt with depression ever since my adolescence," he said in a *New Yorker* profile. "Moving into some periods, which were debilitating, when I found it hard to get off the couch, to periods when I was fully operative but the background noise of anguish still prevailed."[9]

For fifty years he tried just about everything to deal with his depression: booze, drugs, sex, religion. In his late fifties he became a monk and spent six years meditating at a Zen center on Mount Baldy in California. Nothing worked, so he left. In his poem "Leaving Mt. Baldy," he wrote, "I finally understood / I had no gift / for Spiritual Matters. / 'Thank You, Beloved' / I heard a heart cry out." He sent this note to Roshi, his master: "I'm sorry I cannot help you now, because I met this woman."[10]

In 1999, he went to Mumbai, India, to study with Ramesh Balsekar, a former banker and Indian spiritual guide. Whether it was related or not, his depression lifted. He said the background of anguish that had been with him his whole life began to dissolve. By then, he was in his mid-sixties. "There was just a certain sweetness to daily life that began asserting itself," he recalled. "Wow, this must be like everybody feels. Life became not easier but simpler."[11] Cohen claimed the cure was simple: he learned to ignore himself. It seems his longing for that other love also returned. The legendary ladies' man wrote this self-deprecating homage to Indian women: "India is filled with many exceptionally beautiful women who don't desire me. I verify this every single day as I walk around the city of Bombay. I look into face after face and never once have I been wrong."[12]

❧ Love at Second Sight   MARLENA BLAVIN

A second look can lead to true love.

When bodywork therapist Marlena Blavin first heard the voice of her future husband, David Roche, she was behind a curtain. His voice gave her goose bumps. They were both volunteers, learning how to give massages to terminally ill patients at a medical center in San Francisco. "I was entranced by his voice," she recalled. "It stirred something in me."[13] She fantasized him as her ideal man, with thick curly brown hair, piercing dark eyes, and olive skin. When he stepped from behind the curtain and she saw him, she walked away without saying a word. "I had never seen anyone who looked like David," she said in an interview.[14] She was referring to the left side of Roche's face, which is marked by repeated surgeries and radiation burns as doctors dealt with the huge benign tumor that he was born with.

Blavin's curiosity quickly overcame her shock and embarrassment. "There was something about him that kept me taking another look," she said. "I kept watching him during the class. I was attracted to his sense of humor, the bold way he spoke," she said. "David just has this magnetic way about him."[15] She asked to be his massage partner. It became Blavin's way of looking beyond Roche's face and touching his soul. They became friends. Months later, they fell in love.

Their educational video, *Love at Second Sight*, tells the story of their romance and eventual marriage. It's a story of perception—of shifting one's gaze, of following one's heart, and of discovering and accepting our inner beauty. The video is designed to help young people who are on the verge of puberty deal with the challenges of appearance and acceptability, although the teachers and parents who watch it are just as attentive. In the video, Blavin describes her initial confusion with openness and gentle humor. In the discussions that follow, she and her husband model dealing with the judgments of others and not going along with the crowd. "That first look is not what counts. I needed time to adjust to David's face and how he looked," she says. "David needed a second look and a second listen. I needed a second look. We all need a second look."[16] "We were like two sleeping beauties who woke each other up," she said in an interview.[17] David agrees. As he said in an interview, "Perhaps true beauty is something that draws our attention at second glance, once the judgment of a first glance has realized its mistake."[18]

✃ Sex and the Gimpy Girl NANCY MAIRS

Intimacy and desire are ageless.

When American writer Nancy Mairs's husband of thirty-five years became impotent, her mother told her she could live without sex. "I know I can," Mairs replied. "I just don't want to."[19] She and her husband, George, both had infirmities, he from cancer, she from multiple sclerosis. "Desire doesn't arise down there but up here," she wrote in her essay "Sex and the Gimpy Girl." In her book *Waist-High in the World*, Mairs wrote, "If we demanded enchantment, we'd be sorely let down."[20] She wrote frankly about a life that people might have trouble imagining but might experience one day. For example, they might assume that a sexual relationship cannot be sustained when one partner provides routine care to the other. It's just not true, she said. Even though her and her husband's bodies held "few mysteries for each other," the routine of caregiving didn't diminish their attraction. "Once you've helped your wife change her wet pants, or watched the surgeon pop a colony of *E. coli* from the healing wound in your husband's belly, you have seen behind all the veils."[21] She explained that her husband's impotence had a physiological rather than psychological basis and didn't usually discourage them from lovemaking. In fact, "because we have grown so familiar with each other's physical realities, we love each other more unabashedly and inventively as time goes on."[22]

Mairs felt that having her husband participate in her care called her into life. "To view your life as blessed does not require you to deny your pain," she wrote in her book *Carnal Acts*. "It simply demands a more complicated vision, one in which a condition or event is not either good or bad but is, rather, both good and bad, not sequentially but simultaneously."[23]

◈ Crossing Half of China to Sleep with You
YU XIUHUA

Passion is the essential provocateur.

Chinese poet Yu Xiuhua has been compared to Emily Dickinson. Her poems are about love and erotic longing. One of them, "Crossing Half of China to Sleep with You," has been read by millions of Chinese people and made her the voice of a rising feminist movement in her country. The lines include the following:

> *To sleep with you or to be slept, what's the difference if there's any?*
> *Two bodies collide—the force, the flower pushed open by the force,*
> *the virtual spring in the flowering—nothing more than this,*
> *and this we mistake as life restarting.*[24]

The *New York Times* selected Yu Xiuhua as one of the most courageous women in the world in 2017. She has a reputation for not backing down from a fight, whether it is against being labeled a peasant poet because she lives and farms in rural China or being labeled a disabled poet because she has cerebral palsy. She recently got into a spat with the elder statesman of Chinese poetry, Guo Lusheng, who didn't like her description of a perfect afternoon: drinking coffee, reading a book, and making love. He felt she should be writing about the miseries of rural life. Her defiant response was that she never felt life in the countryside was all that miserable and that perhaps his real criticism was that she insists on holding her head high despite "being on the bottom rung of society."[25]

Yu Xiuhua was forced into a marriage to a older man when she was nineteen. They have one son, who is now in university. Her parents did the arranging because they feared she would never be able to take care of herself. Their marriage was loveless. She began writing poetry at twenty-seven, saying she needed to do something to keep her spirits up. In her poem "I Am Not Alone" she wrote, "I believe what he has with others is love. It's only with me that it's not."[26] Once she became famous, she used her book royalties to buy her husband a separate house. Then she divorced him. She now lives with her father in a newly built two-story house. *Still Tomorrow* is a documentary about her rise to fame and her refusal to live a life without love. Poetry, says Yu Xiuhua, is her spiritual walking stick when she is stumbling around in life. "Without poetry, life is empty. When I write, I feel poems give me peace and tranquility."[27]

✎ Fifty Shades of Scarlet MIK SCARLET

Sex is much more than penetration.

Mik Scarlet woke up one morning when he was a teenager and found he couldn't walk. His spine had collapsed in his sleep, the side effect of treatments he had received for childhood cancer. He has used a wheelchair ever since. "There was no more standing for me," he joked to a TV audience. "And there was also no more standing to attention down there."[28] Scarlet was no longer able get an erection. Not the kind of news a teenager wants to hear.

Scarlet became a singer-songwriter influenced by punk and Goth culture. To give you a sense of his flamboyant personality, he named one of his bands Scarlet Messiah. Today he is a UK media personality, the first disabled presenter to work on mainstream national TV, and the first disabled actor to appear in a soap, where he was described as "Wheelie Sexy." He was recently listed as one of the most trusted journalists in the UK. Scarlet also co-hosts "The Love Lounge," which offers online advice on sex, love, and disability. "Sex is something we all want and we all have a right to enjoy," he says.[29] He bills himself as a nonexpert expert. Scarlet is happily married to Diane Wallace, the former lead singer in one of his bands.

He believes that society needs to move away from a freaky image of disability and sex. One reason is because anyone can become disabled. "When I incurred my spinal injury, I thought my sex life was over," he said, "but nothing could beat the sex I have now."[30] With the help of a group of lesbian friends, he learned how to make love to a woman, like a woman. They even made him an honorary lesbian. "I know that sex is so much more than penetration," he said in an interview. "You can make somewhere else your erogenous zone, for instance, if you don't have sensation in your genitals anymore."[31] Scarlet writes and produces videos introducing people to the expanded world of sexuality that he discovered. He advises people to think themselves to orgasm and offers advice on finding orgasmic zones on their body—for example, inside the mouth or on the shoulder. "There is so much ignorance," says his wife, Diane. "People assumed our sex life was over because Mik was disabled. But there was a raw sexuality about Mik; he was so easy and confident."[32]

✿ Things Disabled People Know about Parenting ING WONG-WARD

The natural act of parenting shouldn't have to be a radical act.

Award-winning broadcaster Ing Wong-Ward decided to become a journalist at the age of thirteen after a friend won an award for being her "savior." The friend had been profiled by a local reporter. Upon seeing how she was portrayed, Wong-Ward decided she could write a better story about disability in general.

Wong-Ward, who died while this book was in production, was born with spinal muscular atrophy, a neuromuscular condition. She always used a wheelchair and needed personal support care to live her life.

As a result, she grew up used to people's stares. She thought she had learned to live with them. However, she was unprepared for the frozen look she received from a drugstore cashier when she wheeled up to the counter to pay for a pregnancy test. At that point, she knew she was in for a variety of judgments that most pregnant women don't face.

While many of her medical practitioners offered support, there were some who assumed she would be a less than competent parent. A head nurse in the neonatal department where she delivered her baby wrote a detailed note about Wong-Ward's disability, adding nothing about her day-to-day life. Knowing that so many disabled parents face additional scrutiny after having their babies, Wong-Ward wrote a detailed letter outlining the supports that she and her husband, Tim, had in place. Their daughter, Zhenmei, has since grown into an active preteen who was once wheeled around town on the back of her mom's wheelchair.

Wong-Ward was married to her university sweetheart, Tim Wong-Ward, for more than twenty years. During this time, she faced invasive questions about her family life. In response, she tweeted this reply to #ThingsDisabledPeopleKnow: "Yes. The baby is mine. Yes. She is my bio child. No. I did not use a surrogate. No. I did not need invitro. No. I did not consider aborting her when I found out I was pregnant. No. I would not have aborted her if I had found out she had a disability."[33]

Wong-Ward believed that giving birth to her daughter was probably the most radical thing she had ever done. "I recognize that by having her and being her mother in public, I'm making a major statement about a whole bunch of things: about being a disabled woman, about sexuality, about reproduction," she said in an interview.[34]

Wong-Ward went on leave from the Center for Independent Living in Toronto after being diagnosed with inoperable cancer. She received palliative care to manage a variety of symptoms. She and her husband were frank with their daughter, explaining that while Mom was going to die, the family would remain strong. They expected they would have lots of time to be together and create memories.[35] Sadly, in the summer of 2019, Ing Wong-Ward passed away peacefully from complications of colon cancer with her husband by her side. Her daughter was able to give her mom a final kiss

✎ In Sickness and in Health BEN MATTLIN

Shared intimacy means fewer pretenses.

When writer Ben Mattlin was a college student, he was kissed like he had never been kissed before. Unlike most male college students, he hadn't taken the initiative. He couldn't scratch his nose, let alone walk. He had to ask his girlfriend, Mary Lou, to kiss him. Sparks flew. "You weren't aggressive, but you had a hunger that was sexy," his wife recalled. "And yet I knew I was safe with you. It was only going to go as far and as fast as I wanted, which was something I needed at the time."[36] They've been together for more than thirty years and have two children.

Mattlin describes himself as an opinionated 120-pound New York Jew who prefers to talk. He uses a motorized wheelchair and is unable to pick up a pencil or feed himself because he has a neuromuscular condition called spinal muscular atrophy. His wife is a California Protestant who reflects before talking and prefers to act. She wanted a house with a backyard. He was a city boy. Disability seemed the least of their differences. Yet the fact that he has disability and his wife doesn't still seems odd to other people. Mattlin wrote his latest book, *In Sickness and in Health*, to explore the reasons why society finds romance between a person with a disability and a person without one so strange, yet accepts interfaith, interracial, and same-gender couples. That's why he coined the word *interabled*.

Strangers assume that his wife must be his nurse, sister, mother. That he's a burden and she must be a saint. That he's lucky to have her. "I simply fell in love with a guy who happened to be in a wheelchair.

Nothing noble or self-sacrificing about it," Mattlin quoted Mary Lou in an interview.[37] He believes the emotional, financial, and physical challenges that interabled couples face are similar to what other couples eventually face as they age. "There's a shared intimacy that many interabled couples enjoy that I think other couples really would envy if they understood it," he said in an interview. "You know the other person's vulnerabilities early on. And once you learn to not be afraid of that and trust each other, you can actually emerge a stronger couple than you might have without that."[38] Especially if your wife gets the house with the backyard!

Did You Know . . .

The website Sexuality and Disability (https://sexualityanddisability.org/) updated the Kama Sutra to include twenty-four sexual positions for people who have physical disabilities and limitations.

Did You Know . . .

The hashtag #DisabledPeopleAreHot is used by people with disabilities to proclaim their sexiness. The hashtag's creator, Andrew Gurza, who hosts the podcast *Disability After Dark*, wants disabled people to celebrate being sexual and sensual and nondisabled people to move past their biases and preconceptions.

❧ LESSON 5

All Means All

Every single one of us—woman, man, gay, straight, disabled, perfect, normal, whatever—is powerful when we are not trying to fit in, when we are not leaving half of ourselves outside the room. —CAROLINE CASEY

Our challenge for the future is how to make relationships and build organizations based on the realization that there is no one whose contribution we do not need.
—JACK PEARPOINT

I also see the value in creating a world that caters to the needs of the whole spectrum of humanity.
—RICHARD BRANSON

❧ What Ted and Josh Kuntz Taught Me

DIVERSITY STRENGTHENS OUR social immune system. It is key to creating more resilient and caring communities. This is why Jeff, one of two teachers who were dividing seventy students into two grade-seven classes with the toss of a coin, picked Josh Kuntz.[1] "I don't understand," said Mike, the other teacher. "Why would you choose a child with severe disabilities as your first pick?"

"Well," said Jeff, "I think having Josh in my class will make it a kinder and gentler place for everyone. I've been around the school for a number of years, and I noticed how the other children responded to Josh. I noticed they were eager to greet him when they passed him in the hallways. I noticed children modifying games to include him and comforting him after a seizure."

73

Josh was Ted Kuntz's son. The story of the two teachers dividing seventy students into two grade-seven classes with the toss of a coin is the centerpiece of Ted's book *Peace Begins With Me: An Inspirational Journey to End Suffering and Restore Joy*. It's a story I never got tired of hearing as Ted rehearsed in front of a few of us before hitting the road to speak about the importance of diversity. Josh was born healthy but acquired a disability early in life due to the aftereffects of a vaccine. He was left with an uncontrolled seizure disorder. It affected his intellectual development and his language. Josh could speak some words with difficulty, but few people could understand them. That didn't matter to Ted and his wife, Cathy Anthony: they requested, indeed insisted, that Josh attend the same neighborhood school as his sister.

And it didn't matter to Jeff, the teacher who chose Josh because he understood the multiple benefits of inclusion. He knew Josh would benefit from being in a regular classroom. He also knew Josh would enrich the learning environment for his classmates, make the school a better school, and make him a better teacher. Jeff once told Ted that he believed Josh's ultimate contribution was teaching his classmates how to become caring citizens. Ted's corporate clients wanted those kinds of benefits too. They wanted to do something more than follow diversity guidelines. They wanted to create a welcoming environment for all their employees, and they believed there was no better way to get started than by inviting Ted to tell Josh's story.

The expressions "Don't put all your eggs in one basket" and "Variety is the spice of life" are reminders that diversity has been a source of strength and renewal through the ages. Nowadays the rhetoric about diversity is everywhere. Diverse viewpoints give us a competitive edge. They stimulate new ways of thinking. They help break logjams. They can lead to breakthroughs. These are true. But only if everyone is included, not just a select few, and if they are welcomed wholeheartedly the way Jeff welcomed Josh. There is still hard work to be done if we are to fully benefit from diversity. Too many people continue to be excluded economically and socially.

The people I've chosen for this lesson know how to make diversity stick so that it benefits both the individuals being included and the wider society. They teach us that you can't be a little bit pregnant or a little bit diverse. One is a pioneer in the corporate field of diversity. Another is refreshing a seven-hundred-year-old tradition of inclusion that is becoming a model of health care and social care reform. Some are demonstrating the benefits of catering to people with disabilities as customers and employees. Others are transforming the fields of fashion, dance, and entertainment.

My wish is that you get to experience the power of the Joshes of this world and commit to using your power and know-how not only to include but also to welcome. Or that you get to be one of the Joshes of this world, recognized for your attitude, skills, and talents and no longer unwisely overlooked.

⋙ The Elephant in the Room CAROLINE CASEY

If disability is not on your agenda, neither is diversity.

Caroline Casey is an Irish social entrepreneur and adventurer. She claims her parents used Johnny Cash's song "A Boy Named Sue" as the inspiration for not telling her that she was legally blind. They wanted to toughen her up. She didn't find that out that she had ocular albinism until she applied for a driver's license. Casey describes her vision as similar to looking through glasses smeared thick with vaseline.

She hid her disability from her employers when she started to work and from most of her friends. She didn't want to appear weak or to ask for help. One day an eye specialist asked her, "Why are you fighting so hard not to be yourself?" she recalled in a TED Talk.[2] It was a defining moment. She eventually left her job and decided to pursue a childhood dream to become Mowgli from *The Jungle Book*. She became the first female mahout (elephant rider) from the West to trek across India on an elephant. Her journey was filmed by National Geographic in the documentary *Elephant Vision*. "It's extraordinary how far belief can take you," she said.[3]

Since her return from India, Casey has used that belief to address society's elephant in the room, the inclusion of people with disabilities in business. In industrialized countries, only 20 percent of people with a disability are employed. In developing countries, it is significantly less.[4] Casey believes that business is the only force on the planet capable of remedying this inequality crisis. "We know that if business values disabled people equally, then society will too," she said in response to the results of a survey of attitudes of business leaders to disability inclusion.[5] She wrote in June 2019 that "despite 90% of companies claiming to prioritize diversity, only 4% actually consider disability."[6]

In 2019, she made history at the World Economic Forum's annual summit in Davos. She launched "The Valuable 500," a call to action for five hundred global business leaders to put disability issues on their board agenda. "It's no longer good enough for companies to say 'Disability doesn't fit with our brand' or 'It's a good idea to explore next year.' Businesses cannot be truly inclusive if disability is continuingly ignored on leadership agendas," she said.[7] Some of the biggest brands in the world have signed on, including Unilever, Microsoft, Barclays, Fujitsu, Sainsbury's, Bloomberg, Boeing, Cinépolis, and Accenture. Paul Polman of Unilever and Richard Branson of Virgin were the founding Valuable 500 leaders. "After more than five decades as an entrepreneur and investor, I know firsthand how valuable different perspectives are in every aspect of business," said Branson. "Any business not engaging with [people with disabilities] is doing its customers a disservice."[8]

Casey wants to change the world for everyone. That's why the Valuable 500 uses the term "diversish" to caution against being selectively diverse and only including some people with diverse backgrounds and experiences depending on what suits the company best. Their cheeky two-minute film *Divers-ish* won a bronze award at Cannes Lions for effective marketing communication.[9] Casey wants a world where everyone belongs. "Inclusive businesses will create inclusive societies," she says. "Diversity is not about prioritizing one group over another. It's about all groups."[10]

⚘ Krip-Hop Nation LUCA PATUELLI

The hip-hop community dances to inclusion.

There are many reasons why hip-hop has replaced rock and roll as the most popular form of music. For one, it combines rapping, sampling, deejaying, guerrilla art, fashion, and break dancing. For another, its roots are in social critique and protest. Hip-hop is more than entertainment—it is a way of thinking, a way of turning the status quo on its head and reconfiguring it. Hip-hop may also be the world's most inclusive art form. And Luca Patuelli, aka Lazylegz, is one of its stars. He is lead dancer with the Théâtre National de Chaillot in Paris and has his own dance crew, which tours the world. Growing up, he felt insecure and blamed his disability for his not being able to do things. Discovering dance gave him the opportunity "to use my difference as a strength and not look at it as a weakness," he said in an interview.[11]

Patuelli was born in Montreal and raised in Bethesda, Maryland. He has a muscle condition that affects the bones and joints of his body, which required sixteen surgeries before he was seventeen. He uses crutches when he walks. He dances with and without them. "The beauty with breaking and hip-hop is being unique," he explained in an interview. "There are a lot of movements I'm physically not capable to do because of the way my legs were born and because of my shoulders, but I am able to create my own unique style using the strength of my arms."[12]

His crew of eight dancers with disabilities is called ILL-Abilities. Hip-hop regularly flips a negative term and turns it into something positive. Thus "bad" is "good" and "ILL" means "very cool." ILL-Abilities includes Tommy "Guns" Ly, who had his right leg amputated as a teenager. Ly is attracted to hip-hop because while there are guidelines, there are no rules. "I've had to be clever and creative, expanding the possibilities of what I can do with just one leg," he said in an interview.[13] Another crew member is Jacob "Kujo" Lyons, who hears music as a static drone. He compensates by memorizing and following the visual clues of other dancers. "There's an unexpected freedom in not being able to hear," said Lyons. "I can dance independently of the music, meaning my movements are off-beat, figuratively and literally."[14] ILL-Abilities also includes South Korea's Jung Soo "Krops" Lee, who broke his neck in a dance injury in 2013. He was told that he would never walk again, but he says they neglected to say anything about dancing. "After my injury, I wanted to break down the wall between normal people and handicapped people," Lee said, "and have everyone have the same possibilities to do everything."[15]

ILL-Abilities "has become a brotherhood," Patuelli said in an interview. "It's beyond dance."[16] He said one of his roles is to bridge the gap between dance and hip-hop to make the world a more inclusive and accessible society for all. "Dance is the connection between you and the universe; while we are dancing we are developing ourselves based on the energy, the emotions, and the challenges we experience," he said in the Canadian Dance Assembly's 2015 International Dance Day message.[17]

Note: To learn more about the intersection of hip-hop and disabilities around the world, check out the website Krip-Hop Nation.[18]

✃ Runway to the World AARON PHILIP

Diversity is more than a fashion.

Aaron Philip tweeted her modeling career into existence when she was seventeen. Her tweet read, "honestly when i get scouted/discovered by a modeling agency it's OVER for y'all! by y'all i mean the WORLD!"[19] Less than a year later, she became the first disabled, gender-nonconforming, trans woman of color to sign with Elite Model Management. That's the company founded by John Casablancas. Shortly after, she landed her first magazine cover with the *Isis Nicole Magazine*. Aaron (pronounced "ay-ron") has cerebral palsy. She uses she/her pronouns and a wheelchair to get around.

Philip has always been determined. "Sometimes, it's you who has to trigger your own happiness," she told her online followers.[20] She wrote a memoir at age fourteen titled, *This Kid Can Fly: It's About Ability NOT Disability.* It tells the story of immigrating to the Bronx from the island of Antigua with her family, who wanted better medical options for her, and living for two years in a homeless shelter because of large medical bills. The lack of diversity on the runway deeply affected her as she was growing up. It drove her to take matters into her own hands, "to carve a space and try to provide opportunity for members of my community in this field. And while this might sound inspiring to some, to me it's simply a matter of showing the world something different, and opening people's minds—especially in fashion, where there's a fine line between art and consumerism."[21]

Fashion is important to her because "it's the ultimate form of conveying self-expression and toying with gender."[22] Her ambition to become a model was accelerated by a magazine cover that pictured model Kylie Jenner posing in a golden wheelchair. Jenner does not have a disability. The portrayal made Aaron determined to shift the image of disabled people from fetish to muse. She wants the world to know that muses can be black, physically disabled, and trans. "It is no longer enough just to be a pretty face," said Susannah Hooker of Elite Model Management. "Models also have a social responsibility, as they are increasingly becoming influencers, particularly to the younger generation."[23] Philip said in an interview that she thinks the industry has "an obligation to create spaces that are accessible, clean, open, and well thought out for people that aren't able-bodied."[24] She doesn't want it to end with her. Her signature style, confidence, and hustle suggest that it won't.

✃ Unleash Different RICH DONOVAN

Catering to the disability market means
delighting customers with disabilities.

When Rich Donovan started on Wall Street, he wondered whether he could keep up with the speed of its markets. Now Wall Street should be wondering how to keep up with the speed of the market he is a specialist in, the disability market. Donovan knows that it is more powerful than business realizes. The combination of people with disabilities plus their families and friends means that the disability market touches 63 percent of consumers. "This is not a niche market," he said during a speech in 2019.[25] It's a market that amounts to $8 trillion in annual disposable income, $645 billion in the United States alone. Aging baby boomers will add to those numbers as they acquire disabilities, he adds. His book *Unleash Different: Achieving Business Success Through Disability* outlines the details of the world's largest emerging market and how organizations can grow revenue and cut costs by attracting people with disabilities as customers and talent.

Donovan was a portfolio trader at Merrill Lynch for eight years. As far as he knows, he was the only one with a visible disability. He has cerebral palsy and wondered whether people would have trouble under-standing him, so he began using instant messaging and email until they got used to his voice. Donovan eventually earned his firm $35 million in profit before he left in 2008 to form the Return on Disability Group. Their slogan is "Translate different into value." Catering to people with disabilities as customers and employees is a business opportunity, he says, not a charitable problem. "Quotas and equity laws do not cause hiring," he wrote in an opinion piece. "It's the promise of future profits that does."[26] The key, he said in the 2019 speech, is not to design for disability but "to design from disability."[27] Accessibility might get peo-ple in the door, but they have to have a reason to want to. "That means figuring out what you have to do to delight them," he said.[28]

Donovan created the Equity Tracking Indices to recognize public companies that are outperforming in the disability market. They are published daily by the New York Stock Exchange. Their latest annual report notes that "firms with the highest results in disability-driven value creation outperform their competitors in terms of long-term stock price."

✃ Navigating Privilege and Power
DEBORAH DAGIT

Diversity means using your power and privilege to explain
how things work to those who have been excluded.

Deborah Dagit lived for months at a time in a hospital when she was a child, often in a full-body, plaster of Paris cast or with her legs in trac-tion, unable to move. She was born with a genetic condition that caused her bones to break easily and take a long time to mend. It often results in shorter-than-average stature. Dagit is four feet tall. She's had more than sixty fractures, most of them when she was a child. Her single mom lived an hour's drive away. Since visiting hours in the 1960s were much shorter than they are nowadays, they usually saw each other for an hour on Sunday afternoons. On top of that, she wasn't allowed to make phone calls. "I wasn't sick or ill," she said. "Just incredibly bored."[29]

To keep herself busy, she became a keen observer of how hospitals worked from a kid's point of view. She used those insights to make the hospitals less terrifying for others. She requested that the other children's beds be placed near hers. She gave her fellow patients tips on where to get the best food, which nurses were the kindest, and which TV shows were the best. "As my new friend shifted from being terrified to giggling, I became increasingly popular with the medical staff," she said. "It became abundantly clear the universe had put me here to help others."[30] At nine years of age, she had discovered her life's purpose.

She has been helping people navigate institutions and big companies ever since. She describes her journey as similar to scaling Mount Everest. Even though she had a college degree, she was taken aside by several HR leaders at her first entry-level job and told that "someone like her was lucky to have a job and should not waste others' time applying for bigger roles."[31] Once she was flown to New York, put up in a nice hotel, and picked up in a limousine for an interview with a Fortune 50 company. When the recruiter saw what she looked like, he told her that she wasn't what they had expected and promptly canceled the interviews. On another occasion, a human resources executive told her that having her work at his company would be like a heart transplanted into a body that rejected it.

Dagit persevered. She became a pioneer in the diversity field, leading initiatives in three Fortune 200 firms. She became the first diversity leader who identified as a person with a disability. Dagit said in a keynote speech that her privilege and her power are defined by her vulnerability, not by her title, rank, or wealth. It gives her an insider's perspective on how workplace cultures work for people who have been excluded. "Regardless of our age and station in life, all of us can be leaders if we acknowledge and share the knowledge we uniquely have to help other's paths become easier," she said.[32]

✥ Sharing Lives

THE VILLAGE OF GEEL AND ALEX FOX

A seven-hundred-year-old approach to inclusion is transforming health and social care systems.

Since the fourteenth century during the Renaissance, the Belgian village of Geel has been a sanctuary for people labeled mad, crazy, insane, or mentally ill. It was so well known that Vincent van Gogh's father considered sending his famous son there. Seven hundred years later, Geel families are still being hospitable and setting the norm for non-medical, community care. The host family is not told anything about their new boarder's diagnosis or background. It's left to the individual to decide how much to tell them and when. Families are simply expected to share their lives and to make their boarder feel part of their family. Many boarders spend the rest of their life with successive generations of one family—for example, first as a daughter, then a sister, and finally an aunt. "They are part of the family—we love them," said Toni Smit in an interview. She is from one of Geel's host families.[33] Philippe Pinel, the founding father of French psychiatry, observed that "the farmers of Geel are arguably the most competent doctors; they are an example of what may turn out to be the only reasonable treatment of insanity and what doctors from the outset should regard as ideal." Oliver Sacks, the poet laureate of contemporary medicine, was equally enthusiastic. "Unimaginable elsewhere! I would like to see more places like Geel," he said in an interview.[34]

Geel's deeply personal approach to care is enjoying a renaissance in the UK, thanks to the organization Shared Lives Plus. They support ten thousand host families who welcome more than fourteen thousand people into their homes. Everyone benefits. Their CEO, Alex Fox, observes in his book *A New Health and Care System: Escaping the Invisible Asylum* that the families will move heaven and earth for people they regard as friends and family, not as clients. Shared Lives is making waves as a practical alternative to costly and impersonal health and social care. Compared with professional care, the quality is consistently high and the turnover is low, as is the cost. Fox writes, "The act of sharing your home and family life is radical, even shocking in a world where we can feel we have less and less contact with each other, but it's also deeply personal."[35] It gives modern meaning to the phrase, "It takes a village."

❧ An Authentic Doctor DAVID RENAUD

People are looking for real stories about
real people from diverse backgrounds.

A motorcycle accident at the age of nineteen left David Renaud paralyzed. He became a doctor to find a cure for spinal cord injuries, only to realize that he loved being a storyteller more. So he left family medicine and earned a screenwriting degree from UCLA. Today he is executive story editor for the hit TV series *The Good Doctor*. The fact that he uses a wheelchair makes him a better doctor and a better writer, he said in an interview. "When you have a disability, you always need to work harder to prove that you can do the job as well as everyone else, which means you have to be better than the average person."[36]

The Good Doctor focuses on the demands of medical training, including burnout and bullying. Its main character, Shaun Murphy, played by Freddie Highmore, is a young surgeon with autism. Renaud's aim is to normalize the idea of a doctor with a disability, something he is an authority on. "Show society the world you want often enough and people will start to see the world that way," he said. "Then, the barriers will come down."[37]

Renaud thinks that one of the reasons *The Good Doctor* has been a hit with viewers is because they are telling real stories about real people. "Autistic, blind, deaf, wheelchair users—we're all part of this big community of people who are struggling to have our stories told. And not just told, but told in an authentic way," he said in another interview.[38]

ஜ All Means All

MARSHA FOREST AND JACK PEARPOINT

Everyone belongs.

You can't be a little bit pregnant. And you can't be a little bit included. Either you are in or you're not. Those are the beliefs that led educators Jack Pearpoint and his late wife, Marsha Forest, to breathe new life into the term *inclusion* in the late 1980s. It was a heady time in the disability world. Segregated schools and separate classrooms were closing. Students with disabilities were being mainstreamed and integrated. There was a three-letter hitch, however—the word *but*. "It was being used to exclude far too many students," said Pearpoint. "All means all," he added.[39]

The messaging from school boards was similar: Of course all children are welcome in our schools and classrooms . . . But, we don't have enough money. But, we aren't trained. But, there is no curriculum. But, not those children with those kinds of disabilities. The "buts" kept coming despite the availability of money, training, support, curriculum, and evidence that all children benefit when children with disabilities are included in regular classrooms.

In frustration, Pearpoint and Forest invited a group of colleagues and disability advocates from across North America to their Toronto offices. The topic was what to do about the "buts." By the end of the meeting, they agreed that the word *inclusion* best conveyed the principle that everyone belongs, no buts about it. The idea embedded in the word took off. It continues to be nurtured by Inclusion Press, a publishing house they established, and an annual Summer Institute in Toronto, which Pearpoint hosts with Lynda Kahn, his wife and partner. Inclusion isn't a program or something one "does to or for someone else," Pearpoint has said. "It's a way of thinking, a deeply rooted spiritual concept that one lives."[40]

Did You Know . . . the Montessori Method

Italian doctor and educator Maria Montessori developed her innovative teaching methods working with children who had developmental disabilities. These methods changed the way we educate all children. She believed that intelligence wasn't fixed and that it could be enhanced by a stimulating environment and by nurturing a child's natural desire to learn. Montessori was the first educator in the world to use child-sized tables and chairs in her classrooms. She pioneered open classrooms, early childhood education, educational toys, and the idea that children learn through play. "It is not true that I invented what is called the Montessori Method," she said. "I have studied the child; I have taken what the child has given me and expressed it, and that is what is called the Montessori Method."

Adversity Is an Opportunity

I think that the only true disability is a crushed spirit; a spirit that's been crushed doesn't have hope, it doesn't see beauty, it no longer has our natural, childlike curiosity and our innate ability to imagine.

—AIMEE MULLINS

It may seem hard to believe, but it's catastrophe that offers the most promise for an even richer life. This is the gateway to the good stuff. In other words, you never truly know which way the wind is blowing until the shit hits the fan.

—MICHAEL J. FOX

℘ What Sam Sullivan Taught Me

MANY OF THE world's most enduring advances have come from people whose love in the face of adversity was so strong that they had no choice but to rise again. And again and again.

If Sam Sullivan hadn't decided to get into politics, he could have become the king of gizmos. (He defines gizmos as one-of-a-kind customized devices and gadgets that make life easier for people with disabilities.) Instead he became mayor of Vancouver. He remains a well-known British Columbia politician.[1] Sullivan's inventiveness emerged out of darkness. He broke his neck in a skiing accident at the age of nineteen. All the things that had meant so much to him, like music and sports, no longer seemed possible. He struggled with depression for years. In the depths of his despair he considered ending it all. As he played out the details in his mind, he found himself thinking of those he loved, particularly his young niece. By coincidence, she visited him the next day, greeting him with her usual "Hi, Uncle Sam!" It was a watershed moment. He decided to stop thinking about what he was missing and to live his life with gusto. He resolved to do whatever was necessary to make that happen. What started as self-preservation led to breakthroughs that have spread far and wide, affecting people inside and outside the world of disability.

Traveling with Sullivan always turns me into an apprentice. I remember one road trip from Vancouver to Oakland, California, to visit Jerry Brown when he was mayor of the city. It was an exercise in collecting the scraps of paper that Sullivan doodled on. Or scribbling on scraps to write down another one of his bright ideas. Sullivan can't help himself. He's a modern-day Leonardo da Vinci. Ever curious, he is constantly thinking of ways to eliminate the barriers that prevent people from getting to know each other and helping each other out.

His innovations include a suite of organizations to assist people with spinal cord injuries who want to fly ultralights, play and record music in a fully accessible studio (he named his own band Spinal Chord), sail boats simply by sipping and puffing with their mouths, and garden at wheelchair height. He also helped invent the TrailRider, a one-wheeled vehicle that enables people with spinal cord injuries to travel in the backcountry. It's been used to reach the base camp of Mount Everest. Sullivan's ingenuity lives on in the Tetra Society, which has unleashed a network of gizmo inventors across North America. It matches volunteer engineers, technicians, and designers to people with disabilities who have an accessibility challenge. He also played a leadership role in generating public support for the first safe injection site in North America, a decade before anywhere else, and established a "greeting fluency" initiative to teach people how to greet people from other cultures in their own languages.

Adversity can be our teacher if we let it. And why shouldn't we? Sooner or later, it will find us. And we have to decide what to do with it. Conquer it? Hide from it? Fight it? Leave it to others? Often we have no choice but to accept it. Acceptance isn't resignation or giving in. It's an acknowledgment of reality, of what exists. Acceptance gives us a base to begin figuring out what to do next. Adversity appears in a variety of forms: accident, loss, hardship, cruelty, destruction. Whether it happens to us or to someone or something we love, the suffering and pain is deeply personal, at times unbearable. Grief, anger, fear, and despair are understandable reactions to adversity. So too are the opportunities that people find. This is not to gloss over anyone's misfortune or to suggest that they are solely responsible for addressing the situation they find themselves in. They are not. A person's adaptive, problem-solving capacity is enhanced by a caring network and access to resources.

Adversity calls forth our ingenuity. We must do something because no one else is or will. Justice burns brightly. We try anything, borrow anything, cobble together anything at any hour of the day and night until something works or somebody does something. We act with a focus and creativity that we never thought we had. Adversity also cracks us open. We see the world as it is, not as we thought it was or want it to be. We embrace its complexities, contradictions, and ugliness, with a determination and love that we never thought possible.

The people profiled in this lesson treat adversity as an opportunity. While it may not be the opportunity they wanted, it's the one they have been presented with. They have made use of their suffering and hardship to find common ground with others, often making improvements that have benefited many others.

My wish is that we find the natural strength that exists within each of us. That we find meaning in our struggles and losses. That we don't treat them as personal failings and that we don't shut ourselves off from others. As Sam Sullivan discovered, adversity may be the mother of invention, but love is another parent.

❦ Mothering On CHRISTA COUTURE

Resilience is born from suffering and reflected in celebration.

Singer, songwriter, storyteller, and self-described cyborg Christa Couture is no stranger to grief and loss. Her left leg was amputated when she was thirteen as a cure for bone cancer. Then her two baby boys, Emmett and Ford, died for different reasons, one at a day old, the other at fourteen months. In between, her father died. Later there was a divorce. Recently she had two surgeries on her neck—the first to remove a thyroid cancer, the second to address an arterial bleed that erupted shortly after and which threatened her singing voice and her destiny, a destiny that was foretold by the indigenous elder who, in honor of her mixed Cree heritage, gave her the traditional name of Sanibe, which means "singing woman." "Grief is a very lonely feeling, and so getting to make songs about it and share those songs was a way that I could be less alone," she told a radio interviewer. "It's how I have survived the hardest parts of my life."[2]

Despite her candor, Couture is careful about what she shares publicly. She simply knows there are parts of grief that naturally reveal themselves to others. So she makes those parts beautiful through her songs and blog posts. The rest remains private. Her philosophy might be summed up by the advice that a drag queen once gave her: "If you can't hide it, decorate it." A good example was her decision to post pictures of her recent pregnancy. Not seeing any pictures of pregnant women with disabilities online, she made her own. It was the first time she had taken off her state-of-the-art prosthesis for a photo. The leg, decorated in a floral fabric, leans against the wall as she sits cross-legged, looking directly at the camera. The pictures went viral. "I knew people might do a double take, because they've only been fed images of certain bodies," she said. "But we need to normalize these differences."[3] She hopes that other disabled women will come across her images and feel that their difference is powerful. "Go get all glowy with your pregnant self," she wrote. "Whatever body you're in."[4]

Although the surgeries changed her voice, Couture is still singing. And she is learning to celebrate. "I don't just accept my disability—I can celebrate it."[5] She says she had become so focused on not letting her pain be swept under the rug in our get-over-it culture that she forgot to shine a light on her joys and many accomplishments—which include becoming the mother of a baby girl, hosting a radio show, and writing her new book, *How to Lose Everything.* It is scheduled to be published in late 2020. "It's not that it gets easier, but it does change," she says.[6]

◈ Breathing Love into Zika
THE *GUERREIRA* MOTHERS OF BRAZIL

Love and adversity are a powerful combination.

In the lead-up to Brazil's 2016 Summer Olympics and Paralympics, the world's gaze was fixated on what the media described as the horror and tragedy of congenital Zika syndrome (CZS). They portrayed Brazilian parents and their babies as grieving victims. They used the images as a backdrop to discuss the herculean challenge that Western science has to overcome to eradicate the virus. In doing so, the journalists missed another gaze—the look of love in these same parents as they fussed over their babies.

They also missed the determination of Brazilian parents, particularly moms, to rise to the occasion. These parents consider their children a blessing even though they face tough challenges and strains, including the demonization of their babies. They know that science and technology can't solve every problem, and that they distract attention and deflect resources that should be available to support these families.

Brazilians with disabilities and their families receive limited government support. So a group of mothers who have had babies with CZS created United Mothers of Angels (UMA) to share information, referrals, and treatment, and to make sure their children are not forgotten.

They call each other *guerreiras* (warriors). Germana Soares is their leader. "We are protesting so that this generation of special needs children will not be rendered invisible. Our babies are citizens, they have rights, and while they cannot speak we are their voice," she said in an interview.[7] Germana's son Guilherme has already exceeded the predictions of doctors. He is starting to speak. "He has a really strong personality, he is very strong-willed," said Soares. "He knows what he wants and when it's a no, it's a no."[8]

Debora Diniz, a Brazilian anthropologist and lawyer, and author of *Zika: From the Brazilian Backlands to Global Threat*, described these mothers as "the domestic scientists who have been key in advancing our understanding of CZS" in an interview. She said they are guiding the "white coats and biomedical groups."[9]

Ꮼ Radical Optimist HELEN KELLER

Adversity demands justice.

Mark Twain said that Helen Keller would be as famous a thousand years from now as when she lived. It wasn't for the reasons most people think. What they know about Keller has been fashioned by the film *The Miracle Worker* and its two remakes. They know that a mysterious illness when she was a baby left her unable to see, hear, or speak, and that her teacher Annie Sullivan helped her learn how to read and write. Twain understood that there was more to Keller's story. He was impressed by her intelligence, quick wit, and commitment to justice and equality.

Keller was a popular lecturer and writer who became known as the socialist Joan of Arc. "I, too, hear the voices that say 'Come,'" she wrote, "and I will follow, no matter what the cost, no matter what the trials I am placed under. Jail, poverty, calumny—they matter not."[10] She campaigned for women's and workers' rights and an end to racial segregation. She was an early advocate of birth control. She was a cofounder of the American Civil Liberties Union (ACLU). She wrote a series of essays on socialism called *Out of the Dark*. Keller believed that it was an unjust economic system that kept people with disabilities and others poor and unemployed. Her radical politics led to public criticism. Some newspapers criticized her by drawing attention to her disabilities, suggesting that her "mistakes sprung out of the manifest limitations of her development."[11] She even drew the attention of the FBI, which suspected she might be a communist because of her radical ideas. She wasn't. Later in her life, she became a successful diplomat, representing the United States in post–World War II Japan.

Keller's optimism wasn't the cross your fingers and hope for the best kind. It was a learned optimism that emerged from the experience of adversity. She wrote in her journal, "Character cannot be developed in ease and quiet. Only through experience of trial and suffering can the soul be strengthened, vision cleared, ambition inspired, and success achieved."[12] She advised people to hold their head high and look the world straight in the face. "For imagination creates distances and horizons that reach to the end of the world," she wrote in *The Story of My Life*. She added, "It is as easy for the mind to think in stars as in cobble-stones."[13] Keller received the Presidential Medal of Freedom in 1964.

๛ Adversity Is an Opportunity AIMEE MULLINS

The ability to adapt is a key survival skill.

If Aimee Mullins can change her legs, she thinks the least you can do is change your mind—about disability and adversity. She's no stranger to either. Both her legs were amputated below the knee when she was a year old, due to a condition she was born with. She has twelve different pairs of prosthetic legs, changing them depending on the terrain, and whether she is running, going out for the evening, or simply wanting to change her height. Some she describes as wearable sculptures. She jokes that half of Hollywood has more prosthetic in their body than she does but we don't think of them as disabled.

Mullins first attracted media attention for her athletic achievements when she set world records in the one hundred meters, two hundred meters, and long jump. Today she is better known as a fashion model—the face of L'Oréal—and as an actress, including playing Eleven's mother on the Netflix series *Stranger Things*. She is also one of the reasons why Chris Anderson purchased and transformed TED Talks into a global phenomenon. Her three TED Talks have been viewed more than seven million times.

Mullins is regularly asked to speak about overcoming adversity, which makes her uneasy. She says adversity isn't about triumph over tragedy, or about overcoming a challenge, unscathed. "It's just change we haven't adapted ourselves to yet," she says in her TED Talk titled "The Opportunity of Adversity."[14] It changes us physically and emotionally. And our responsibility is not to shield our loved ones from adversity; it's to prepare them to meet it with confidence and creativity.

Adversity is inevitable, she suggests. The question isn't whether we will meet it but how. Seeing it as "natural, consistent, and useful" means that "we are less burdened by its presence."[15] She paraphrases Charles Darwin: "It's not the strongest of the species that survives, nor is it the most intelligent that survives; it is the one that is most adaptable to change."[16]

⚭ Better and Darker Angels ABRAHAM LINCOLN

Making peace with darkness makes us wiser.

Abraham Lincoln is considered one of the greatest US presidents. The challenges he faced have been well documented. They included the death of his eleven-year-old son, Willie; an apparently loveless marriage; and the terrible death and discord of the Civil War. He also experienced clinical depression. In those days it was called "melancholy." When Lincoln was in his twenties, neighbors occasionally took him in for fear that he might take his own life. His law partner observed that "his melancholy dripped from him as he walked."[17]

According to Joshua Wolf Shenk, author of the book *Lincoln's Melancholy: How Depression Challenged a President and Fueled His Greatness,* Lincoln's depression "lent him clarity and conviction, creative skills in the face of adversity, and a faithful humility that helped him guide the nation through its greatest peril."[18] Lincoln's open-heartedness and humanity derived from integrating the polarities of darkness and light in his own life. He didn't separate Americans into two camps, North/South, victor/vanquished, or good/bad. He urged "an awe-inspiring sense of love for all" in his second inaugural address.[19] In his first inaugural address, Lincoln said, "We are not enemies, but friends. We must not be enemies. Though passion may have strained, it must not break our bonds of affection. The mystic chords of memory will swell when again touched, as surely they will be, by the better angels of our nature."[20]

⚏ Image Maker FRANKLIN DELANO ROOSEVELT

Adversity expands the heart.

The reason that the image of President Franklin Delano Roosevelt (FDR) is on the American dime is because he founded the March of Dimes. In 1938, he encouraged people to donate by forming a march of dimes all the way to the White House to help find a cure for childhood polio. Dimes came by the truckload—2,680,000 dimes, or $268,000, in the first month. Jonas Salk benefited from the donations and eventually developed the polio vaccine. The American public had a general sense that

Roosevelt had polio because he had retired temporarily from politics. Few understood that he was paralyzed below the waist and could not walk on his own when he returned. That's because he stage-managed his appearances. On his first inauguration day, he rolled to the stage in his wheelchair, hidden by a barrier. Then he walked the last few steps, supported by one of his sons. He had hand controls in his cars so that he could be seen driving, and he banned people from taking pictures of him with his braces, wheelchair, or canes. Roosevelt felt the camouflage was essential because the designation "cripple" would have caused the erasure of a politician of that era.

Ironically FDR's disability prepared him to lead the American people through the Depression, World War II, and the implementation of the New Deal. His secretary of labor, Frances Perkins, watched FDR's long period of rehabilitation, which began in 1921 when he was thirty-nine. "The man emerged completely warm-hearted, with a new humility of spirit," she said.[21] His wife, Eleanor, said that polio had made her husband more sensitive to the pain of others and determined to do something about it. Roosevelt was much blunter. "Once you've spent two years trying to wiggle one toe, everything is in proportion," he said.[22]

Roosevelt's New Deal faced stiff opposition. It was criticized as either creeping fascism or closet communism, and as too much, too soon. Roosevelt persisted and was reelected in a landslide. One of the strategies his administration employed was nurturing the arts. The result was an outpouring of creativity that reflected the sentiments and values of New Deal policies. "I, too, have a dream," wrote Roosevelt in a 1938 letter, "to show people in the out of the way places, some of whom are not only in small villages but in corners of New York City . . . some real paintings and prints and etchings and some real music."[23]

Roosevelt's success at political image making has meant that the allure of the New Deal lives on. Sadly, so does the effect of his personal image making, which hid his disability. The headline of an article written by Roosevelt's grandson Curtis in 1998 reads, "FDR: A Giant Despite His Disability."[24] That is why advocates with disabilities ensured that the statue placed at the entrance to his memorial in Washington, DC, in 2001 shows him seated in a wheelchair. It was paid for with private money raised by the National Organization on Disability. Inscribed on the plaque is this quote from Eleanor Roosevelt: "Franklin's illness . . . gave him strength and courage he had not had before. He had to think out the fundamentals of living and learn the greatest of all lessons—infinite patience and never-ending persistence."[25]

✍ Breaking Ground PEARL S. BUCK

Adversity gives birth to social movements.

Pearl S. Buck's first book, *The Good Earth*, was published in 1931. It went on to become a classic of American literature. It won the Pulitzer Prize and helped Buck to become the first American woman to win the Nobel Prize in Literature. The novel tells a story about the struggles of Chinese peasants during a period of drought before World War I. Wang Lung, the main character, has a child with a disability whom he loves and cares for throughout the starvation and hardships of peasant life.

In 1950, Buck broke new ground again when she wrote *The Child Who Never Grew: A Memoir*. The title reflects the diagnosis she received when her daughter Carol was born, a diagnosis she never accepted. During that era, parents who refused the advice of doctors to place their child in an institution and go home and forget about him or her were left in what Buck described as "private and sacred isolation." Newspapers refused to let parents place ads seeking other parents who had children with disabilities. Buck explained that she started writing because she needed extra money. "For I knew all too well the cost of lifelong care for such a child. . . . I was well paid as teachers go, but now I had to earn much more."[26] The money she earned from *The Good Earth* paid for several years of her daughter's schooling.

Pearl Buck's decision to write about her daughter Carol helped give birth to the family arm of the disability movement. There is a direct connection between her and small groups of families who were banding together to advocate for their children throughout Europe, Australia, New Zealand, and North America. That included the Kennedy family. John F. Kennedy's sister Rosemary had an intellectual disability. When he became president, he established what is now the President's Committee for People with Intellectual Disabilities. JFK's sister Eunice Kennedy Shriver helped found the Special Olympics. Collectively, this international movement of families persuaded the UN to create a Declaration on the Rights of Disabled Persons in 1975. It was the first UN Declaration of any kind. Buck said that placing her daughter in a school affected her for the rest of her life: "I don't know of any blow in all my life that was as rending. It was as if my very flesh were torn."[27]

✂ The Dark Side of the Game TIM GREEN

Some things in life are costly. Others are priceless.

Tim Green made his reputation tackling opposing quarterbacks for the NFL's Atlanta Falcons. He then became a successful broadcaster and writer. In 2016, he was diagnosed with ALS (amyotrophic lateral sclerosis), also known as Lou Gehrig's disease, named after the New York Yankees baseball star, who also had ALS. Green believes his ALS is the result of the constant blows to his head that he received as a defensive lineman for the Atlanta Falcons. He lost track of the number of concussions he suffered. "I used my head on every play. Every play. Every snap. It was like throwing myself headfirst into a concrete wall," he said in an interview.[28] He said that he might not have developed ALS if the current regulations that limit helmet-to-helmet contact in practice and penalize it in games had been in place. He believes football has taken ten to twenty years off his life.

Green made his diagnosis public on CBS's *60 Minutes* when he could no longer hide his symptoms. Denying pain and injury was a survival strategy that worked for him when he was playing football. "I'm a strange guy," he told an NPR interviewer. "I get something in my head and I can just run with it. I was really afraid I had ALS. But there was enough doubt that I said, 'All right, I don't. Let's not talk about it. Let's not do anything.'"[29] Green was ambivalent about whether playing football was worth it. "Can I say getting ALS was worth it? I don't know. I don't know."[30] He pointed out that most people who play football don't get ALS.

Green is determined to maintain the positive attitude that he has had all his life. "So whenever the end point is," he said, "I ask to be strong enough to maintain that positive attitude no matter what the challenges are."[31] After leaving football, Green became a best-selling author. He is writing his thirty-ninth book with a sensor on his glasses that he uses to point at letters on the computer. He said he wants to continue being the best dad, lawyer, writer, and businessperson he can be. "I don't know anyone more fortunate and blessed than me—even with this," he told *60 Minutes*.[32] Green's memoir is called *The Dark Side of the Game: My Life in the NFL.*

Note: Tim Green is one of a growing number of football players who have been diagnosed with ALS. The NFL's current concussion settlement acknowledges the link between countless head collisions and ALS. It includes payouts for former players who have ALS, including Green.

Did You Know . . . the First Bicycle Was a Wheelchair

In 1655, Stephan Farffler, a Nuremberg, Germany, watchmaker, invented a three-wheeled device called a *manumotive carriage*. It is believed that Farffler either had a spinal cord injury or had had his legs amputated. He moved the carriage by turning a hand crank attached to the front wheels. It was the first self-propelled wheelchair and the forerunner of the tricycle and bicycle.

Did You Know . . . Hand Signals in Baseball

Hand signals in baseball were devised by William Hoy in the late 1800s. Hoy was a center fielder who holds the record for throwing three runners out at the plate in a single game and hitting the first-ever grand slam home run in the American League. He was also deaf. He had to ask his coaches whether a ball or a strike was called. While awaiting their answer, the pitcher often sneaked in a quick pitch, striking the batter out before he was ready to swing. Hoy devised hand signals that the third base coach could use to relay the umpire's call so that he could keep his focus on the pitcher.

Nowadays, more than one thousand silent instructions are given during a regular nine-inning baseball game.

Art Blooms at the Edges

I hope that the power of art can make the world more peaceful.
—YAYOI KUSAMA

My interest is that the art that is presented should not be through the filter of "disability"; I would like it to be appreciated as art, and you don't have to like it. —GEOFF MCMURCHY

People seem to worry about self-expression that is somehow too personal. Art has always been personal. —BONNIE SHERR KLEIN

℘ What Geoff McMurchy Taught Me

GOOSEBUMPS NEVER LIE. The inescapable truth of making the world a better place is that we must touch hearts before we appeal to minds.

Geoff McMurchy and I were protesters together for years.[1] Placards, rallies, political confrontations, and late-night strategy sessions were commonplace. Those were the early days of disability activism. In contrast to most of us, Geoff dressed elegantly, his hair and beard neatly trimmed. He was gentle, unfailingly polite, although determined. He could wheel through crowds with the agility of a skater. Midnight calls from him were routine. There was a lot to do, and Geoff was good at it—the complete advocate. Except his heart was elsewhere.

He had been a dancer before he broke his neck in a diving accident. It became clear that he still was when he wheeled onto center stage with his sister Shannon to perform their dance creation *Wingspan*. They dove and swirled around each other and around the stage—she on the tips of her toes, he in his chair, arms extended by shiny metallic wings emblazoned with feathers that he had sculpted. They soared. And so did we. They danced us to the end of limitation and into imagination. I had goose bumps. Many of us cried. Of course we noticed his chair; how could we not? He used it the way a poet uses words. And of course Geoff and his chair couldn't fly. No one can. But we can soar by imagining the world we want and by creating art that takes us there. Which is what this dancer in advocate's clothing did for the rest of his too-short life. Leaving the advocacy business to others, he became the artistic director of a festival that continues to shine the spotlight on artists with disabilities.

The beauty created by artists with disabilities is not a frill, a nice-to-have, or personal therapy. It's both a necessity in itself and necessary in order to change the world. The signs of an evolving consciousness within any movement appear first among its artists. That's because artists specialize in making feelings, hunches, uneasiness, and desires visible. Like Geoff, they excavate memories and link them to imagination. Too many of the conversations about personal and social change are wrapped in the terminology and jargon of psychology, economics, politics, science, and technology. While this language can be useful, it is limited in describing the caring world we want for ourselves and for others, and limited in attracting the support we will need to get there.

Artists with disabilities are developing language, symbols, and images based on the experience of disability. They are making sense of longing, outrage, and despair. They are reminding people that they are not foolish or stupid. Their edginess is generating pride, nurturing celebration, and illuminating purpose. And they are creating a vibe that alerts others to pay attention—that it is time to catch up. The explosion of poetry, dance, drama, music, sculpture, and painting among people with disabilities is more than an assertion of competence and capability. It is proof that disability is cool.

The people profiled in this lesson remind us that we shouldn't ever part with anything that makes us human. They are using art to bridge the silos that divide us, to help us taste life, and to entertain us. Some even manage to find beauty and purpose among nastiness, obliteration, and desecration. They all know that the artist's struggle is the activist's struggle. They work at the edge, rallying the downhearted, brokenhearted, openhearted, and bravehearted.

My wish is that we never separate the dancer from the dance. That we welcome the artists in our midst, including artists with disabilities. They are indispensable companions on the social journey because their wingspan is so much greater.

❦ Art Blooms at the Edges YAYOI KUSAMA

Art beautifies what we dread.

The first pumpkin that artist Yayoi Kusama saw was growing on a farm she was visiting with her grandfather when she was eleven. When she went to pick it up, it began speaking to her. She made a painting of it and won a prize. Eighty years later, one of her large silver pumpkin sculptures sold for half a million dollars. The sources of Kusama's sculptures, paintings, and writings are the obsessional images that she has experienced since childhood.

Kusama left Japan to escape an abusive family and a Japanese culture that was "too small, too servile, too feudalistic, and too scornful of women."[2] She was an integral part of the 1960s avant-garde scene in New York. The painter Georgia O'Keeffe was her business adviser. She became friends with Andy Warhol and influenced his painting style. Her mission was to democratize art. In her autobiography, she wrote that her "commitment to a revolution in art caused blood to run hot in my veins and even made me forget my anger."[3] However, her hallucinations and panic attacks were increasing in intensity. In the early 1970s, she left the United States and returned to Japan.

She checked herself into a psychiatric hospital in Tokyo, where she still lives. Every morning, she leaves and crosses the road to her studio, where she continues to create. She views her paintings as diary entries and connected to her illness. The art world forgot about her for decades. A retrospective show in 1989 just before the fall of the Berlin Wall turned things around. Today she is the most popular artist in the world, as calculated by the number of people who attend her installations in museums and art galleries. *Time* magazine named her to its "100 Most Influential People" list. In 2018, her artwork netted more than $108 million at auction.[4]

Kusama is called the "priestess of polka dots" because she paints polka dots on everything. She says it is her response to the waves of infinity and nothingness that threaten to dissolve her. "If there's a cat, I obliterate it by putting polka dot stickers on it. I obliterate a horse by putting polka dot stickers on it. And I obliterated myself by putting the same polka dot stickers on myself," she said in an interview.[5] Kusama is now in her ninth decade. She still wears bright red wigs and polka dot dresses and uses a polka-dotted wheelchair. Her most famous installations are mirrored constructions titled *Infinity Room*. Inside the room are glowing polka dots, orbs of every size, changing colors and floating silently. They encompass the visitor. They invite you to ponder the mysteries of the universe. Kusama wants us to feel humbled. "Our earth is only one polka dot among million of stars in the cosmos," she said in a documentary about her work.[6] She wants us to appreciate our place in the universe. "Forget yourself. Become one with eternity. Become part of your environment."[7] And she wants us to be comforted. "Far beyond the reaches of the universe, infinity is trying to communicate with us."[8] We leave feeling more connected. Her hope becomes ours. At the opening of one of her exhibitions, she said, "I think I will be able to, in the end, rise above the clouds and climb the stairs to heaven, and I will look down on my beautiful life."[9]

✆ The Heart of the Matter ITZHAK PERLMAN

Art is medicine that helps us forget the harshness of life.

Itzhak Perlman taught himself to play the violin on a toy instrument when he was three because his hands were too small. Today he is a violin superstar. People describe his playing as praying with the violin. He's won sixteen Grammys and received the Presidential Medal of Freedom. He has been a regular on *Sesame Street*. He plays all styles of music from klezmer to jazz to fiddle. He has played bluegrass with John Denver, backed up pop singer Billy Joel, and performed the violin solos for the movie *Schindler's List*. *Itzhak*, the musical documentary about his life, was nominated for a 2019 Grammy. The secret of his success: "One must always practice slowly. If you learn something slowly, you forget it slowly."[10]

Perlman was diagnosed with polio when he was four. As he began playing in public and making TV appearances, people would say, "Very nice, not bad for someone who is disabled." They treated his playing of Rimsky-Korsakov's "Flight of the Bumblebee" on *The Ed Sullivan Show* when he was thirteen as a novelty act. Nowadays they tell him he's heroic. His reply: "Look, I had polio when I was four. So when you're four years old, you know, you get used to things very, very quickly."[11] Perlman uses crutches or a scooter to move around and plays his violin seated. He says that many soloists wish they could sit too. Besides, he says in the documentary *Itzhak*, "I don't play the violin with my legs. I play it with my hands."[12] He wants people to be moved to tears by his music, not his polio—although, he says, getting around isn't getting any easier. For that reason, "I always champion anything that will improve the lives of people with disabilities and put it on the front burner."[13]

Beauty is good medicine, he says. "You forget the harshness of what's going on when you experience music in a concert hall."[14] Perlman's perseverance is illustrated in a *Houston Chronicle* story about a 1995 concert that Perlman performed at Lincoln Center in which he broke a string at the beginning and played the whole concert with three strings:

> We were all on our feet, screaming and cheering, doing everything we could to show how much we appreciated what he had done.
>
> He smiled, wiped the sweat from his brow, raised his bow to quiet us, and then he said—not boastfully, but in a quiet, pensive, reverent tone—"You know, sometimes it is the artist's task to find out how much music you can still make with what you have left."[15]

✿ Black Beauty ANNA SEWELL

Protest literature can be beautiful.

When Anna Sewell, the author of *Black Beauty,* was fourteen, she was seriously injured in a fall. She used a crutch to help her move around. For longer journeys, she relied on horses, which opened her eyes to the inhumane treatment they suffered. Sewell wrote *Black Beauty* to "induce kindness, sympathy, and an understanding treatment of horses."[16] The book also encourages people to treat each other with respect. Sewell has one of her characters say, "My doctrine is this, that if we see cruelty or wrong that we have the power to stop, and do nothing, we make ourselves sharers in the guilt."[17]

Published in 1877, her *Autobiography of a Horse* contains detailed passages on how to care for horses. It was largely thanks to *Black Beauty* that England passed laws abolishing the mistreatment of horses. It outlawed the "bearing rein," a strap that pulled the horse's head down toward its chest, causing pain and respiratory problems, all for the sake of creating a beautiful arch.

Black Beauty was Anna Sewell's only book. She wrote it in bed in the last few years of her life when she was in her fifties and in declining health, the lingering effects of her childhood injury. She died five months after the book was published, without knowing that it would become so popular. It has since sold fifty million copies and is the sixth-best-selling book in the English language. She was paid twenty pounds for writing it.

✎ The Key of Life STEVIE WONDER

Music unifies, making the world more loving and inclusive.

Singer and musician extraordinaire Stevie Wonder used his voice to earn more Grammy awards than any other solo artist. He also won an Academy Award for best song with "I Just Called to Say I Love You," the Polar Music Prize, and the Montreal Jazz Festival Spirit Award. He is one of the first artists to secure his artistic freedom by writing, producing, arranging, and performing his own songs. *Songs in the Key of Life* is his best-selling and most critically acclaimed album. In an interview, he said that he never thought of his blindness as a disadvantage in the same way that he never thought that being black was a disadvantage. "I am what I am. I love me! And I don't mean that egotistically—I love that God has allowed me to take whatever it was that I had and to make something out of it."[18]

Wonder is also using his voice to make the world more inclusive. He was a strong advocate for ending apartheid in South Africa. He was instrumental in the campaign to make Martin Luther King Jr.'s birthday a US national holiday. In fact, he put his career on hold for three years to lead rallies in support of the idea. "As an artist, my purpose is to communicate the message that can better improve the lives of all of us," he told a crowd in Washington, DC, in 1981.[19] The first official

Martin Luther King Jr. Day was January 20, 1986. It was celebrated with a concert, headlined by Wonder. He asked the crowd, "If we cannot celebrate a man who died for love, then how can we say we believe in it?"[20] Since 2009, Wonder has been a United Nations Messenger of Peace, with a focus on people with disabilities. "The more people who are doing things that make a difference and are part of this world of inclusion," he said, "the smaller the world gets of people who are not committed, and ultimately we will end up with a world of inclusion."[21]

✎ A Chair in the Sky

CHARLES MINGUS WITH JONI MITCHELL

Artists push limits in search of freedom.

Jazz bassist, pianist, and composer Charles Mingus was a musical prodigy. He became a jazz legend because racial discrimination and poverty prevented him from pursuing a career in classical music. The Library of Congress has placed his music scores beside those of Mozart and Beethoven. Mingus defined creativity as making the complicated simple, whereas most people did the opposite and made the simple complicated. Mingus said that creativity was more than being different and that he was "going to keep on getting through, and finding out the kind of man I am, through my music. That's the one place I can be free."[22]

Mingus developed ALS in 1977. It began with a weakness in his arms and legs, and then it affected his speaking, swallowing, and breathing, which prevented him from playing. He continued to compose by humming the melodies and instrumental parts into a tape recorder. His last project was a collaboration with singer-songwriter Joni Mitchell. She was diagnosed with polio as a child and developed her unique style of tuning during her recovery because her left hand had been weakened. Mitchell recalled in an interview that Mingus liked the fact that she was musical adventurer like him, willing to push the limits. Mingus viewed the album as his epitaph. He asked Mitchell to take his music and add lyrics that would express his final wishes.

The album was called *Mingus* when it was released in 1979 shortly after his death. Today it's better known as *Chair in the Sky*, after a song on the album that Mitchell composed in honor of Mingus. When she first met Mingus, he was sitting in his wheelchair in his Manhattan high-rise. She imagined him as a king sitting on his throne. "He was a very commanding figure," she recalled.[23] In her memoir, *Tonight at Noon*, Mingus's wife, Sue Graham Mingus, wrote of a conversation they had near the end of his life, when he said, "Next time I want to be a star. I want to be flashing all night long. A star stays up there till it burns out and becomes something else."[24]

✂ Outsider LUCY MAUD MONTGOMERY

The imagination cannot be contained.

Lucy Maud Montgomery is the author of the world-famous *Anne of Green Gables* stories. Unlike her heroine, she did not have a charmed life. Her mother died when she was two, and her father remarried. She didn't like her stepmother, and her father sent her to live with her grandparents. They were strict and not affectionate. Montgomery acknowledged in later life that the imaginary friends and places she developed to escape her loneliness and isolation also developed her creative mind.

The Green Gables series made Montgomery a household name around the world. They are about the adventures of an orphaned red-headed, freckled eleven-year-old girl who's been sent to the Green Gables farm in Avonlea, Prince Edward Island, by mistake. The books have sold fifty million copies worldwide and have been translated into thirty-six languages. In 2016, the online magazine *Slate* declared Anne the patron saint of female outsiders. Author Margaret Atwood wrote that what distinguished *Anne* from so many "girls' books" of the first half of the twentieth century was its dark underside. She added that Montgomery wrote as "a way of coming to terms with a deep underlying sadness."[25]

Montgomery's personal life was full of challenges. It included the death of her infant son, criticism for being a woman writer, the clinical depression of her husband, and constant quarrels with her book publisher. "When I am writing I am happy for I forget all worries and cares," she wrote.[26] Montgomery experienced depression herself. "I'm possessed body and soul by this oppression," she wrote in her journal. "They say women shouldn't write; some days I almost give up. But I cannot contain my imagination. I made Anne real. I gave her my love of nature, my love of books, and my childhood dreams."[27]

In 2008, on the one-hundredth anniversary of the publication of *Anne of Green Gables*, Montgomery's granddaughter Kate Macdonald Butler revealed that her grandmother had been isolated, sad, and filled with worry and dread for much of her life. Butler stated that their family wanted to lift the stigma associated with mental illness and "sweep away the misconception that depression happens to other people, not us—and most certainly not to our heroes and icons."[28] The family now believes that Montgomery took her own life.

✂ Equals at Arthur's Round Table

NIALL MCNEIL AND MARCUS YOUSSEF

Art is a medium for bringing out the best in one another.

At first glance, you might think Marcus Youssef's artistic partnership with Niall McNeil is a charitable diversion from true art making. Mc-Neil is a professional actor and playwright with Down syndrome. He isn't the kind of person who writes things down. He prefers to dictate and have others catch what he is imagining, which is exactly what Youssef, winner of the most prestigious theater prize in Canada, does. This pitcher-catcher combo created the play *King Arthur's Night,* an epic interpretation of the Arthurian legend complete with a live band and sixteen-member choir. It has been performed at major festivals in Canada and at the prestigious No Limits, as part of the Hong Kong Arts Festival.

There is no confusion as to who is in charge onstage and off. McNeil never lets you forget it. He didn't just co-write the play. He conceived it, sometimes leads the rehearsals, contributed lyrics to the original music score, and stars in it. "We're ready, we're brave, we're tough, and we can do it," he says.[29] And he does. Youssef plays Merlin to McNeil's Arthur. He is servant, fixer, and rainmaker to the proud but tormented king. It is Merlin's job to help Arthur realize his majestic vision. In real life, Youssef adds structure to the brilliant interplay of McNeil's memory and imagination. McNeil was head-butted by a goat when he was young, so there is a chorus of goats in his Camelot that represent people who have been repressed and excluded. McNeil's genius as an artist, says Youssef, is his ability to subvert expectations and preconceived notions. He makes links between characters and stories that defy traditional categorizations like fictional and real.[30] This is why Arthur's round table is located in Harrison, an hour's drive away from Vancouver, British Columbia, and why there must be fog machines in the play—because there are hot springs in Harrison. "I like to mix stuff around," says McNeil.

In ancient times, Merlin was the most famous practitioner of alchemy, the practice of turning metals like lead into gold. Alchemy was also a symbol of an advanced democracy, a place where everyone's contribution was valued equally. Merlin helped Arthur create the golden age of Camelot. Youssef and McNeil are creating theater along the same lines. They reject the idea that some experiences are marginal and some stories are not worth telling. Creating *King Arthur's Night* meant discovering that every single one of us has things to learn, wrote Youssef in *King*

Arthur's Night and Peter Panties. He said it has led to "one of my most valued and rewarding collaborative relationships, one that demands my fullest presence and deepest, most authentic self." He added that the whole theater troupe quickly discovered that they all had things to learn: "Every single one of us was very good at some things and pretty shitty at others, and that this was equally true for every person in the room."[31] The relationship between McNeil and Youssef attests to their openness and honesty with each other. During a preperformance interview with the two of them, McNeil pointed to Youssef and said, "He talks too much and too fast—that's his disability."[32] The alchemy of creativity is the alchemy of inclusion. McNeil and Youssef know that they need each other and won't fulfill their ambitions without bringing out the best in each other, working together as equals.

❧ Changing the World, One Painting at a Time
YANIV JANSON

Art is activism.

Yaniv Janson is full of surprises. He's a surprise to the art world. Within months of painting his first canvas at the age of sixteen, he was selected as a finalist for two of New Zealand's most prestigious art awards. He is the youngest artist to be invited into New Zealand's Academy of Fine Arts. His work has been displayed in more than forty museums and galleries in four countries, including France. He's a surprise to his family because he paints in bright, vibrant, and happy colors, in contrast to what they describe as his monotone, yes-or-no way of speaking. He's also a surprise to many social activists because he is teaching that art is a powerful tool for social change.

Janson lives in Raglan, a small town on the west coast of New Zealand's North Island. He describes himself as being on the autistic spectrum but prefers to be known as an "art-ivist," who is raising awareness about climate change. "I am one of those people who think they are going to get what they want," he wrote in his book *Changing the World— One Painting at a Time.*[33] He is particularly concerned about the impact of rising sea levels on people who live on or near seacoasts. "My paintings speak for the people yelling for help that nobody hears, even as seas rise to engulf their homes," he said.[34]

Janson has experienced the low expectations associated with people with disabilities. He set out to change that by launching Taking Action, a project to solicit the opinions of New Zealanders with disabilities about the United Nations' Sustainable Development Goals. The UN goals include ending poverty and protecting the planet. He summarized five years of consultation with *Please Do Touch*, a series of installations connecting art, social issues, environmental topics, and disability awareness. The exhibition opened at the United Nations in New York in 2018. Janson encourages people to touch his paintings so they can feel what he feels. "I want to change viewers' relationship to art in a memorable way," he said.[35] "When it comes to humanity's voice, Art and Activism go hand in hand—it's called Art-ivism—and it concerns both you and me," he wrote to accompany his *Please Do Touch* project. "I want to show the world that people with a disability are also passionate about working on the sustainable development goals." And, he wrote on his blog, "If we all play our roles, we can make a better world."[36]

Did You Know . . . Monument to the Holocaust's Three Hundred Thousand Victims with Disabilities

An eighty-foot-long blue glass wall near Berlin's central Tiergarten park and beside the city's world-renowned Berliner Philharmonie concert hall honors the estimated three hundred thousand disabled people who were deemed unworthy of living and were singled out for mass murder by the Nazis.

✆ LESSON 8

Awaken to All Your Senses

We accept reality so readily— perhaps because we sense that nothing is real.
—JORGE LUIS BORGES

I keep vigilant for the unexpected.
—WANDA DÍAZ-MERCED

Knowledge exists beyond accepted logic and reasoning.
—NADIA DUGUAY

✆ What Peggie Taught Me

OUR SENSES AREN'T ORGANS. They are openings. Openings to awareness and knowledge.

My wife and I heard about Peggie from a friend of a friend. They were visiting an aging relative and noticed a young woman living among older people in the extended care wing of our local hospital. "She just lies there all by herself," we were told. Upon investigation we discovered that Peggie had been in a serious car accident when she was two and had been in the hospital ever since, forgotten by the outside world. She didn't speak, spent most of her time in bed, and had no connection with her family. Our advocacy was tested right away. We prevented the hospital from pulling all of Peggie's teeth out. They thought it would be more efficient for staff to feed her. Eventually we were able to get her a properly fitting wheelchair, arrange for her to attend the local high school, and find her a place to live in the community. Through our work at PLAN, we also developed a network of friends who had interests similar to Peggie's, which at the time included the music of Celine Dion and eating.

Diana is one of Peggie's friends. She is also one of the busiest people we know. For years she and Peggie ate lunch together. It had all the deliberate ritual of a Japanese tea ceremony. Diana prepared the lunch in the morning and packed it in a picnic basket along with her antique silverware, crystal glasses, and Limoges china. Arriving at Peggie's new home, she would spread a white linen cloth over the tray on Peggie's wheelchair and set the table. In the gloomy days of winter, they might light candles. First grace. Then the slow savoring of each tasty bite. "Why do you do it?" friends asked Diana. "It's a big chunk out of your week." "Well," she said, "Peggie is the one person I know for certain truly appreciates my cooking. Also it's better than yoga. It's the only time in my life when I slow down. One of Peggie's gifts is her presence. She knows what's good for me."

Our awareness is shaped by thousands of everyday experiences. The more senses we use and the more attentive we are, the better. Combined, they help shape our identity, focus, and well-being, and what we know. They influence the structure of our thoughts, our language, and the way we express ourselves. And they help us sort out what we know to be true as opposed to what we have been conditioned to believe.

There are three shadows that diminish our awareness. The first is that most of us get by with a limited use of our senses. We tend to rely on some more than others—hearing and sight, for example. Even these aren't as developed as they could be because there are multiple layers to each of our senses. It's obvious, for example, that we can hear sounds. As you will soon read, we can also feel, touch, and see sound.

Second, there are invisible forces influencing our awareness. These include fragments of memory, twists of fate, tradition, and the mysterious. They also include intergenerational trauma that works its way into our psyche even if we haven't experienced the abuse and mistreatment ourselves. We don't always appreciate that what's below the surface influences what's above. When we do, we describe it as intuition or a hunch.

The third shadow that affects our awareness is the fact that the way we know and understand the world has been shaped for centuries by rich and powerful people, royalty, clergy, academics, politicians, philosophers, and warriors. It's a vantage point restricted by being in charge and having an inflated sense of superiority. It's not the world. It's one view of the world and not the only view. It's one type of knowledge and not the only knowledge. For example, as a society we are beginning to appreciate that indigenous people have a unique way of knowing based on their relationship with nature and interconnection with all living creatures. People with disabilities also have unique ways of knowing that construct their social reality on their terms, not someone else's. Their relationship to the way the world works, or doesn't, offers a wisdom that has universal application. That's what Diana recognized and appreciated with Peggie's presence.

The people I've chosen for this lesson are more alert to their senses than most of us. For one reason or another they are tuned to the subtleties and nuances of their environment. One has trained her whole body to hear. Another has become a "whole-body-seer." They remind us that our natural state is to be fully alert and that the altered state is the current distracted relationship most of us have with our senses. Most important, they reveal that no single view of the world can occupy all of human space—that disability offers a view of the world that is just as legitimate as the one that comes from wealth and power. This view can liberate us from the excesses of status quo thinking.

My wish is that we become as present and attentive to each other and our surroundings as Peggie and Diana were to each other; that we honor multiple ways of knowing; and that we pay attention to the mysteries and wonders of the world. Awakening to our senses is not just the sensible thing to do—it's essential.

✥ Touching the Rock   JOHN HULL

Blindness is one of the great human states.

Just a few days before theologian John Hull's son was born, the doctors confirmed what he already knew: that he was completely blind. According to his wife, Marilyn, people didn't know whether to congratulate them or commiserate. For the first couple of years, Hull treated his blindness as a problem to be solved rather than a mystery to be explored. He'd do things like tie a string around his foot and attach it to his infant son so that he had a sense of where his son was crawling. Hull, who died in 2015, taught religion at the University of Birmingham and carried on "as a sighted person who couldn't see."[1] In his wife's words, he was in furious denial, continuing to multitask and rush. At one point, he had more than thirty people transcribing hundreds of his taped cassettes.

Eventually Hull hit rock bottom. He could no longer summon the faces of his wife and six children or places he had been—even memories of light. He realized that his subconscious was telling him, "Wake up—this is a crisis—you can't tough this one out. You've got to really face it."[2] He knew that he had to understand his blindness or it would destroy his life. Then something mysterious happened. At the point of darkest despair, his agony, loss, hopelessness, and grief disappeared. He became more intensely aware of his own body and more alert to all his senses than he had ever been as a sighted person. He became a "whole-body-seer." In his book *Touching the Rock*, he wrote, "Being a [whole-body-seer] is to be in one of the concentrated human conditions. It is a state, like the state of being young, or of being old, of being male or female, it is one of the orders of human being."[3]

Hull concluded that sighted people live in a world that is a projection of their sighted bodies. It is not the world, it is only one version. He realized that as a successful scholar he had let false consciousness, false spirituality, and self-deception creep into his life. That it had become too easy for him to imagine life from the top of the pile. He developed a new sense of justice, increasingly conscious of the way that marginalized people experience the world. We must become "more conscious of the long shadows of injustice and oppression which are cast upon us by our linguistic heritage," he wrote in an essay. "Whether the source of this injustice be a patriarchal bias, or a racist prejudice, or an unconscious fear of disability. We must all try to renew, not only the face of the earth, but the face of our language."[4]

Hull kept an audio diary that became his book, *Touching the Rock*. The *New York Times* was so impressed that they commissioned the documentary *Notes on Blindness*. It won an Emmy Award and can be viewed on Netflix. Toward the end of his book, Hull observed, "Blindness is the wrapping, or the medium. The gift lies deeper, on the other side of blindness."[5] His wife, Marilyn, explained in an interview after the documentary was released that the gift her husband was referring to is "living with what is, rather than dwelling with some other imagined existence."[6]

❧ Awakening to Our Senses EVELYN GLENNIE

Our senses are composed of multiple layers.

Scottish percussionist Evelyn Glennie treats her body as a giant ear. She plays in bare feet to feel the vibrations because she has been deaf since the age of eleven. "My innate curiosity led to the discovery that I could use my body as a resonating chamber and sense sound using the whole of myself rather than only using my ears," she wrote.[7] Glennie has won two Grammys and the Polar Music Prize. She has worked with artists as diverse as Björk, Béla Fleck, Bobby McFerrin, Fred Frith, Mark Knopfler, and the King's Singers. She also has a thriving career as a solo percussionist.

Glennie wrote, "We are awakening to the fact that our senses constitute many layers of sub-senses."[8] Hearing is much more than letting sound waves hit your eardrums, she says in the documentary about her, *Touch the Sound*. "It's a specialized form of touch. You feel it through your body, and sometimes it almost hits your face."[9] She illustrates this by describing the whoosh of air we feel when a large truck or train goes by. Glennie feels the vibrations of lower sounds mainly in her legs and feet and the higher sounds in particular places on her face, neck, and chest. In addition, she can imagine sound by watching the movement of a drumhead or cymbal or the flutter of leaves in the breeze. Glennie has said that her deafness is no more important to her than the fact that she is a woman with brown eyes. "Sure, I sometimes have to find solutions to problems regarding my hearing and its relation to music, but so do all musicians," she wrote in an essay on her website.[10] Her awareness of the acoustics in a concert hall is excellent. She describes the sound properties "in terms of how thick the air feels."

Glennie says that losing her hearing made her a better listener and has led to a new ambition: to teach new ways of listening in order to improve communication and social cohesion. "I see a world where we're drowning in sound," she said in an interview. "Even toys are now electronically enhanced, so that they squeak and squawk and beep. There are many layers, and this sound-drenched world is wearing on our patience."[11]

⚭ The Swoon of the Sensuous DJ SAVARESE

Poetry reveals the sensuous.

Poet and essayist David James Savarese (DJ) thinks that poetry is autistic because it "revels in patterned sound," particularly if the patterns are sensuous.[12] In his book of poetry *A Doorknob for an Eye*, he describes autism "as a shroud of ice and dust: beauty's cosmic hen."[13] Savarese coproduced, narrated, and stars in Deej, a Peabody Award–winning film that documents his journey through high school and admission to Oberlin, the Ohio college that was the first to admit women and African Americans. He became the first nonspeaking person to graduate from Oberlin. The film features four of Savarese's poems set to animation. He says, "A poem is like a person wearing earrings: it shimmers in the light."[14] His poem "Swoon" includes the line, "My senses always fall in love: they spin, swoon; they lose themselves in one another's arms."[15]

✷ The Sounds of Science WANDA DÍAZ-MERCED

The ear sees what the eye misses.

Wanda Díaz-Merced is an astronomer from Puerto Rico who hears the stars. She became blind in her twenties due to complications from diabetes. She thought her dreams of becoming an astronomer were over until she discovered *sonification*. Sonification is a way of turning light, and the numbers, graphs, and data it produces, into sound. She now uses her ears to make discoveries that other astronomers miss with their eyes. She says the eyes have limitations because they can absorb only a tiny portion of the electromagnetic spectrum we call light. By hearing the data, she is able to find patterns and phenomena that the eye misses. "What people have been able to do, mainly visually for hundreds of years, I now do using sound," she said in a TED Talk.[16]

Díaz-Merced had trouble finding a job after graduation. She was told there was no such thing as a blind astronomer. Astronomers in South Africa thought differently. They hired her to work at the South African Astronomical Observatory. She currently leads a global project called AstroSense. It teaches sonification techniques to students with and without disabilities. Díaz-Merced also cochairs the American

Astronomical Society's Working Group on Disability and Accessibility. If people with disabilities are allowed into the scientific field, a titanic burst of knowledge will take place, she said.[17]

Thanks to Díaz-Merced, we can now hear and feel an eclipse of the sun using a rumble map, which translates light into touchscreen vibrations. She is also bringing us the music of space. A fellow scientist and jazz musician noticed that the data Díaz-Merced was collecting looked like musical notes. He showed them to his cousin, a musician, who converted them into music that you can listen to on the website Star Songs.[18] When she hears the beautiful symphonic sounds of pulsating stars, Díaz-Merced says, she feels like dancing. "My sight loss has spurred me to develop other ways to observe and study the world—using my hands, my ears, and what some people would call 'physics intuition,' but which I call the heart."[19]

⤞ Labyrinth JORGE LUIS BORGES

Whatever happens, no matter how mysterious,
is a means to discovering who we are.

Poet and writer Jorge Luis Borges was appointed director of Argentina's National Library around the same time as his gradual blindness became complete. He was fifty-five. Even though he loved to read, his blindness gave him a fresh new way of interpreting his experiences. "I speak of God's splendid irony in granting me at once 800,000 books and darkness," he wrote.[20] Legend has it that Borges could tell just by listening how many books were in a bookstore. He invented the literature of "magical realism," which combines mystery, fantasy, and real-world ordinariness. His stories are full of mirrors, labyrinths, shadows, abrupt beginnings, and surprise endings. The stories tilt reality just enough that we are knocked off balance and invited to make sense of our lives in new ways. Suddenly normal isn't what it seems. Suddenly our interpretation of our experience is as valid as anyone else's.

Borges didn't believe in absolute truth, nor that there was a single path to the truth. Instead, it was a labyrinth. "Behind our faces there is no secret self which governs our acts and receives our impressions; we are, solely, the series of these imaginary acts and these errant impressions," he wrote in his book *Labyrinths*.[21] Borges had a positive belief in his readers' ability to interpret the shadows and mysteries in his stories. He encouraged them to gain a better understanding of their reality by taking into consideration forces that didn't appear on the surface, and to legitimize what they might have previously thought was incidental or irrelevant.

Borges felt that his best writing had occurred after he became blind. He described writing as nothing more than a guided dream: "When I think of what I've lost, I ask, 'Who know themselves better than the blind?'—for every thought becomes a tool."[22] In his essay "Blindness," he wrote that everything that happens, including embarrassments, humiliations, unhappiness, and discord, is the ancient food of heroes. They are like clay, "given to us to transform, so that we may make from the miserable circumstances of our lives things that are eternal, or aspire to be so."[23]

Transformer Man NEIL YOUNG

Transformer man . . . your eyes are shining on a beam
through the galaxy of love. . . . Unlock the secrets.
Let us throw off the chains that hold you down.[24]

Pay attention between the lines of rock-and-roller Neil Young's songs, and you'll discover that he has several connections to the world of disability. He had a childhood bout with polio that still affects the left side of his body. Just as his career was taking off, he began experiencing epileptic seizures, a condition that earned him the nickname Shakey. Sometimes the seizures occurred during concerts, and he'd have to leave the stage in the middle of a song. His handlers wanted to keep his condition a secret for fear of tarnishing his image and popularity. Young, on the other hand, wasn't prepared to "keep all this weird polio/epilepsy shit quiet."[25] In his biography, he describes coming out of an epileptic seizure as feeling "like bein' born again and wakin' up and seein' everything is beautiful."[26] Young said, "Did I get songs from the seizures? Probably."[27]

Young has two sons, both of whom have cerebral palsy: Zeke, with the late actress Carrie Snodgress; and Ben, with his former wife, the late Pegi Young. He became a train nerd because of Ben. His song "Transformer Man" captures that shared enthusiasm. Young also wanted the song to convey the challenges Ben faces in expressing himself and being understood, so he used computers and synthesizers to distort the vocals. "He's got his feelings. He's got his sensitivities. He likes life. It's just a condition of life. It's the way he is," said Young in an interview.[28] "If you listen to 'Transformer Man,'" he was quoted as saying in *Shakey*, "you gotta realize, you can't understand the words and I can't understand my son's words. So feel that. For me, even talking about this is very difficult, because I want my children to be able to hear and read what I say and feel loved and know that everything is okay."[29]

ॐ In My Language MEL BAGGS

Language is not just about words.

Writer and artist Mel Baggs has a sophisticated way of expressing herself that most people dismiss, including linguists and scientists. They consider it random, purposeless, and coming from someone who can't think. To correct that impression, she made a video called *In My Language* and posted it on YouTube. It became an internet sensation and attracted the interest of the mainstream media, including CNN's Anderson Cooper. He profiled her, invited her to write a guest blog, and then set up an opportunity for her to answer questions from his viewers. She types at 120 words a minute and uses speech software so that she can keep pace with any conversation and respond in real time.

In My Language is divided into two parts. It begins with Baggs rocking back and forth, flapping her hands, humming, looking out the window, and repetitively rubbing her face in the pages of a book. Part two, titled "In Translation," provides a detailed explanation, via a computerized female voice, of the meaning behind what Baggs describes as her native language. "My language is not about designing words or even visual symbols for people to interpret. It is about being in a constant conversation with every aspect of my environment, reacting physically to all parts of my surroundings. Far from being purposeless, the way that I move is an ongoing response to what is around me," she explains.[30]

Baggs wants to change the assumption that because someone does not express herself in a typical manner, she can't communicate; and because she can't communicate, she doesn't think; and because she doesn't think, she is not a person. That goes for everyone, she says: "autistic and non-autistic, disabled and non-disabled, from all different cultures and backgrounds, and all communication methods," including "the kid in school who isn't taken seriously because she doesn't know a lot of English."[31]

Should autism be treated? she was asked on CNN. "Yes," she typed. "It should be treated with respect." As should anyone whose "language, communication, and personhood are not considered as real as someone else's."[32]

❧ A Little Learning Is a Dangerous Thing
ALEXANDER POPE

Learning is limited if understanding comes too soon.

Alexander Pope (1688–1744) was an English poet who was known for his sharp wit. He is the second-most-quoted writer in the *Oxford Dictionary of Quotations* after Shakespeare. He was a self-taught genius who could understand five languages. He wasn't afraid to express his opinions in public, particularly about the wealthy. "We may see the small value God has for riches, by the people he gives them to," he said.[33] In return, his enemies hit back by describing him as "the most notorious hunchback of the 18th century."[34]

Pope seldom referred to his disability in his writing. One rare example is this: "I cough like Horace, and tho lean, am short."[35] He was four feet six inches tall. Nowadays people suspect he had a form of tuberculosis that affected the growth of his bones.

His *Essay on Criticism* gave us many well-known proverbs: "To err is human; to forgive, divine," "Fools rush in where angels fear to tread," and "A little learning is a dangerous thing. Drink deep, or taste not the Pierian Spring."[36] In Greek mythology, the Pierian Spring was the fountain of knowledge. Pope completed that particular couplet by advising that if we take "shallow" sips from the spring, we "intoxicate the brain" into thinking that we know a great deal. It's only by "drinking largely" that we "sober" up and realize how little we really know.

❧ By and for Equals
NADIA DUGUAY AND EXEKO

Intellectual equality means there are no preconceived notions of who is teacher, who is learner.

Montreal-based Exeko is legitimizing traditional knowledge; street smarts; and the multiple ways people know, create, and express themselves. Cofounder Nadia Duguay describes their process as "intellectual emancipation." They work their magic by assuming the intellectual and cultural equality of people with disabilities, indigenous people, street youth, and people who are homeless. They mediate between the knowledge and creativity emerging from people who live in prisons, squats, subway stations, and homeless shelters and from those who work in universities, libraries, museums, and galleries. In doing so, they embody the meaning of the Latin origin of the name Exeko, *ex aequo*, "by and for equals." "We must directly confront the hierarchy that supports predetermined roles," wrote Duguay in a journal article. "We must re-enchant the world by reinvesting in our ability to recognize, in a spirit of diversity, the possibility of a society in which we are all comfortable being learners—one where there are no preconceived notions of who should be teacher and who student, and one where no people are afraid of losing their own power when others do well."[37]

Exeko staff members roam the streets and back alleys of Montreal offering training in critical thinking. They pair inclusion with poetry and philosophy. They have an "intellectual food truck" that crisscrosses Montreal delivering books and art material. "It is not only food we need. We also want knowledge and wish you to see us as real human beings," said Fabien, one of Exeko's participants.[38] Duguay tells people that their knowledge and creativity are worthy of any university, library, museum, or gallery. Participants agree. "You make my spirit wake up," said one.[39] "I have my own identity again," said another.[40] "If we want to create a world that is more welcoming to all, we must profoundly transform the social norms that govern it, rethink the world by reorganizing what we know about it, and reflect above and beyond what we already know," wrote Duguay.[41]

Did You Know . . . Closed Captioning

In 1972, WGBH, the Boston PBS television station, displayed text at the bottom of the TV screen in order to make their popular show *The French Chef with Julia Child* accessible to viewers who were deaf or who had difficulty hearing. Initially the text was visible on every screen. By 1974, it was available only to those who had a decoder device—thus the term *closed captioning*. Real-time as opposed to prerecorded captioning was introduced in 1982, enabling people to enjoy live events as they happened.

Nothing about Us without Us

. . . given the right circumstances, being different is a superpower.
—GRETA THUNBERG

If the social conditions are disabling, then the culture will be disabling.
—CARMEN PAPALIA

Disability history and culture isn't recognized or documented in our society, and yet we're everywhere. You just have to notice.
—ALICE WONG

℘ What Barb Goode Taught Me

"**LIBERATORS," NO MATTER** how benevolent or loving, can never complete someone else's liberation. That must be done by the person himself or herself.

Just after landing my first full-time job as a disability advocate, I was invited to a national board meeting where I witnessed an intense discussion led by Barb Goode.[1] She was a founder of People First, an organization of people with developmental disabilities who wanted to be recognized as capable of speaking for themselves. Goode spoke softly and plainly. There was an aura of quiet authority about her. It was clear that she wasn't going to back down, however respectful she might be. She and her People First colleagues wanted the board to finance their intervention in a court case to prevent a young woman known as

"Eve" from being sterilized against her consent. Goode said the issue was personal—they feared the same thing could happen to them. To my surprise, many on the board were resistant. These were parent leaders I admired, yet they seemed unwilling to support the request.

Goode and her colleagues eventually received enough support to get started. They spent the next seven years instructing lawyers as the case wound its way to the Supreme Court. The final decision was unanimous. Neither Eve nor other adults with developmental disabilities can be sterilized without their consent. That decision later influenced the UN Convention on the Rights of Persons with Disabilities. The Convention stated that people with disabilities are full persons before the law and free to make their own decisions regardless of cognitive ability.

In the end, that board discussion wasn't about money; it was about the unwillingness of some people to accept that people with developmental disabilities are capable of representing themselves. I didn't know it at the time, but Barb Goode was following a path to democracy that goes back to the 1500s. That was when the phrase "Nothing about us without us" became a motto for political movements that were wresting power from monarchs. A variation of that phrase, "No taxation without representation," planted the seeds for the American Revolution. "Nothing about us without us" was revived by disability activists in the 1990s. The phrase is used nowadays by consumer groups, patient advocates, and populist movements.

The freedom to represent yourself is always claimed, never granted. That's because power is a habit, and few people like giving it up, whether or not they are conscious of their resistance. I've noticed that there are usually three stages to meaningful participation in decisions that affect you. The first is getting a seat at the table, which isn't easy when you don't know that there is a meeting in the first place or haven't been invited. It's no wonder that this stage of advocacy is often characterized by anger and outrage. The second stage is going through the door once it has been cracked open and meeting with the people who, up until then, you considered the enemy. Trust is usually pretty low, particularly in the beginning. Advocates are often haunted by fear—fear that they might inadvertently give something away and let down their constituency. This stage is further complicated if the building and the room are inaccessible. The third stage of representation is having the power to set and influence the policy agenda—an agenda based on your definition of the problem to be solved, not one predetermined by the system or institution. An ally is someone who understands the difference.

The people profiled in this lesson know how to maneuver effectively through these three stages. They've learned the basic ingredients of democratic decision-making, which include exercising power with love, cultivating trust, and laying top-down institutions on their side. Many are accidental activists. One is a powerful politician. They are proof that the disability movement has justice seekers as powerful as Rosa Parks and Martin Luther King Jr.

My wish is that we consider our role as citizen to be just as important as our other roles of worker, consumer, creator, volunteer, friend, partner, and parent. That we regularly flex our democratic muscle and support groups that have been excluded to do the same, even if that means moving to the background. Politics pervades everyday human life. It's not just some things that are about us. Everything is about us. Every one of us.

ᦰ Climate Striking GRETA THUNBERG

Nothing about climate change without young people.

Greta Thunberg began her school strike for the planet in August 2018, skipping school and sitting outside the Swedish Parliament every Friday on her own. Thunberg has said that she is shy and not good at socializing; otherwise she would have started an organization. By the end of the year, she was named one of the most influential teenagers in the world by *Time* magazine. She is described as the moral voice of a generation, a generation that is prompting older generations to take action to resolve our climate crisis. At the United Nations Climate Change Conference in December 2018 she told attendees, "You are not mature enough to tell it like is. Even that burden you leave to us children."[2] Around that same time, she revealed that she had been diagnosed with autism, obsessive-compulsive disorder, and mutism. She credits her autism for her ability to speak clearly and only when necessary.

Thunberg also speaks precisely about the numbers of students, schools, and countries participating in the climate strikes that she initiated. As I was finishing this book, the numbers were 1.5 million students in 2,083 cities in 125 countries. She is equally detailed about the dangers of global warming and climate change. To avoid catastrophe, the world has to reduce carbon dioxide emissions by at least 50 percent by 2030 in order to prevent a 1.5-degree increase in global warming, she says. "We live in a strange world where children must sacrifice their own education in order to protest against the destruction of their future," she told an audience in Berlin. "Where the people who have contributed the least to this crisis are the ones who are going to be affected the most."[3]

Thunberg was bullied at school, so she was prepared for the insults she has received. She has been mocked publicly for her disability. She's been called retarded, a bitch, and a terrorist. "I expected when I started that if this is going to become big, then there will be a lot of hate," she said in an interview.[4] Others have accused her parents of writing her material. Not so, says Thunberg. "My parents were as far from climate activists as possible before I made them aware of the situation."[5] Still others have said that she is too young to be protesting. Thunberg, who was born in 2003, agrees. "We children shouldn't have to do this. But since almost no one is doing anything, and our very future is at risk, we feel like we have to continue."[6]

✃ Independent Living ED ROBERTS

Helping others without making them dependent on you is liberating.

When Ed Roberts applied to the University of California, Berkeley, in 1962, one of the deans responded, "We've tried cripples before and it didn't work."[7] Those were fighting words to a young man who had overcome his fear of being stared at after contracting polio as a sports-loving teenager—who had given up thinking of himself as a "helpless cripple" and saw himself as a star. Roberts was admitted to Berkeley because other administrators overruled the dean. It was 1962, just before the Free Speech Movement made Berkeley into a center for student protests. Other students who used wheelchairs soon followed. They described themselves as the "Rolling Quads." They created the first Center for Independent Living in Berkeley. Roberts became the father of the independent living movement. He described independent living as a psychological idea as much as a physical idea. "We needed to change our attitudes about ourselves," he said in a documentary about him. "Be proud of who we were and what we are, and go out and change things for others and for ourselves."[8]

Roberts said that there was nothing in life if you were not in control of what happened to you. "I'm tired of well meaning noncripples with their stereotypes of what I can and cannot do directing my life and my future. I want cripples to direct their own programs and to be able to train other cripples to direct new programs. This is the start of something big—cripple power."[9]

In 1976, California's governor, Jerry Brown, appointed Roberts state director of rehabilitation, the same department that had refused to help him go to college. He went on to receive a MacArthur genius grant and to create the World Institute on Disability, a think tank on disability policy in the international arena. The secret of his success was working with other people, "moving away from your own problems to help somebody else."[10] He said that helping others liberated him. "It made me a lot freer to help myself."[11]

Roberts died of a heart attack in 1995 at the age of 56. Today there is an Ed Roberts Campus at UC Berkeley. He was inducted into the California Hall of Fame in the same class as Carlos Santana, Magic Johnson, Buzz Aldrin, and the Beach Boys. In 2017, on what would have been his seventy-eighth birthday, he was honored with a Google Doodle. Roberts' wheelchair is now in the National Museum of American History.

✃ Accidental Activist ALICE WONG

Representation without power is not enough to influence policy and practices.

Writer, media maker, research consultant, and proud Asian American nerd Alice Wong attended a White House reception marking the twenty-fifth anniversary of the Americans with Disabilities Act in 2015 using a BeamPro, a telepresence robot that livestreamed her image into a room and enabled the virtual Alice Wong to mix and mingle with those who were able to make it there in person. She was the first person ever to visit the White House in such a manner, making the point that there are many ways to show up and be counted. She said in an interview that she became an accidental activist because she lives in a nondisabled world, "and surviving in it is a full-time activist occupation."[12] She is considered a leader among the current generation of disability activists. For followers who are unable to recognize photos or images, she describes herself as an Asian American woman in a wheelchair who wears a mask over her nose with a tube for her BiPAP machine.

She is the founder and director of the Disability Visibility Project (DVP), a vibrant online community that champions disability culture and history, created in 2014. She is a collaborator and partner in a num-

ber of projects outside of the DVP. She is a partner in DisabledWriters
.com, a resource to help editors connect with disabled writers and journalists, with s. e. smith and Vilissa K. Thompson. Another project in
which she is a partner is #CripTheVote, with Andrew Pulrang and Gregg
Beratan, a nonpartisan online movement encouraging the political participation of people with disabilities worldwide. One of her latest projects is a campaign called Access Is Love, with Mia Mingus and Sandy
Ho. The aim of Access Is Love is to build a world where accessibility is
understood as an act of love and a collective responsibility, not the responsibility of a few individuals. "Almost every group can improve the
way they include disabled people in their movements," Wong said in
an interview. "I'd like to see disabled people present in all movements
and who are in leadership positions with actual power, not tokens."[13]

Wong's activism combines penetrating insight and fierce advocacy
along with a careful attention to the cultural determinants of change.
In that regard, she and her colleagues are reinventing activism for the
twenty-first century. They are countering the negative cultural myths
associated with disability with their own stories. She wrote an op-ed,
"My Medicaid, My Life," published in the May 3, 2017, *New York Times*,
on how this program affects her life and millions of others' as Congress
attempted to repeal the Affordable Care Act. "I resist the idea that representation is enough when what we really want is power," she said in
an interview—power to influence policies and practices.[14] Wong said
that activism comes in many forms and doesn't just mean showing up
at rallies, protests, and marches; online activism is a valuable and legitimate form for people who can't travel or in some cases can't leave the
house. You don't have to march to be in the resistance, she said.[15] She
encourages people to "do what you can, however you can. All efforts
are valuable. And get over yourself!"[16]

Wong edited and published the 2018 e-book *Resistance and Hope:
Essays by Disabled People*, which she called "Crip Wisdom for the People," examining resistance and activism from the perspective of disabled

people. She is the editor of a forthcoming book, *Disability Visibility*, an anthology of essays from 2000 to 2019 by disabled people.

✼ Manifesto for Citizenship CARMEN PAPALIA

*Trust is an essential ingredient of democracy,
and it grows from the grassroots up.*

To performance artist Carmen Papalia, walking is a political adventure that cultivates trust. In *Blind Field Shuttle,* for example, he leads as many as ninety people with their eyes closed, hands on the shoulders of the person in front of them, on an adventure in darkness. They know he is blind and trust that he will lead them safely to a destination of his choice. In *Mobility Device*, instead of using a white cane, he uses the sound of a high school marching band as his navigation system. In *White Cane Amplified*, he walks down unfamiliar streets using a megaphone to ask passersby for their support. He wants to illustrate that the social function of the cane is to prevent people from following their natural inclination to help. Papalia describes himself as a nonvisual learner, a term he chose when a hereditary condition began obstructing his vision. He resists terms such as *legally blind* and *visually impaired*. He views the white cane with its signature red tape as an institutional technology that reinforces dependence and victimhood. The one he uses is made of black graphite and has a wooden handle. "The white cane entrusted a sighted community with my care when all I needed was to be supported in learning through my nonvisual senses," he wrote in an essay.[17]

Papalia puts his faith in mutual support and trusting relationships between people with and without disabilities. His insights also apply to the relationships between all citizens and their democratic institutions. He wants to end the top-down nature of institutions because when you take away the structure institutions are, "just this mess of relationships."[18] He demonstrates this by conducting accessibility audits of art galleries around the world. His aim is for people in power to understand what systemic oppression looks like. It's one thing to be able to get into a museum, he says. It's another to feel unwelcome once you get inside and to encounter exhibits that aren't compatible with the various ways in which you learn. Papalia describes this as a relational approach to accessibility as opposed to the more common rights-based policy approach.

Papalia has worked with New York's Museum of Modern Art, the Guggenheim, the Harvard Art Museums, the Whitney Museum of American Art, Tate Liverpool, and the Vancouver and Ottawa Art Galleries. He wrote *An Accessibility Manifesto for the Arts* to foster a creative, reciprocal, and ongoing relationship between citizens and their institutions. Papalia believes that everyone carries a body of local knowledge and is an expert in their own right; he also believes that interdependence is central to a radical restructuring of power and for leveling the playing field. Accessibility isn't relevant only to people with disabilities, he said; "it is an affirmation of mutual trust."[19]

✂ Disability Rocks HEAVY LOAD

"Nothing about us" means having an ordinary life,
including being able to party late.

The British band Heavy Load was described as "possibly the most genuinely punk touring band today." They are likely the only band in history that had to fight for the rights of their fans to party beyond 9 p.m. The reason: many of their fans were people with learning disabilities and had to leave so that their support staff could be home before their shift ended at 10 p.m. "It's not very punk to go on at 8:30 p.m.," said their bass player, Paul Richards.[20] Since three of the band members also had learning disabilities, they decided to do something about it. They formed Stay Up Late, a grassroots organization working to ensure that people with disabilities could have an active nightlife. Their website proclaims that they believe people with learning disabilities have the right to stay up late and have some fun.

From humble origins in an assisted living project in Sussex, England, Heavy Load played gigs throughout the UK and Europe and even in New York City. They performed at the Glastonbury Festival twice and wrote the theme music for BBC's TV series Cast Offs. The 2008 documentary film Heavy Load boosted their career, even though, as singer-guitarist Mick Williams observed, their music "neither improved nor deteriorated." The reason: "We don't really rehearse much. It destroys our spontaneity."[21] Their last gig was in 2012, when they played London's Trafalgar Square as part of the city's Paralympic festivities. They kept it punk well beyond 9 p.m.

Stay Up Late continues. They have published "A manifesto for an ordinary life," which includes "the right to choose how I spend my time."[22] They also host "(un)Ordinary" conferences where people with learning disabilities and autism tell stories about leading ordinary lives. In 2019, Stay Up Late was selected as one of the top one hundred British changemakers.

Note: In the United Kingdom, *learning disabilities* is the term used to describe people with developmental disabilities.

❧ The Equality Effect FIONA SAMPSON

Human rights law is a crowbar to pry open justice.

Toronto-based human rights lawyer Fiona Sampson has been described as one of the world's women revolutionaries along with feminist activist Gloria Steinem, former presidential candidate and US secretary of state Hillary Clinton, and American diplomat Isobel Coleman. Sampson said in an interview that she remembered challenging the stigmatization, discrimination, and inequality she was experiencing from the time she was able to speak.[23] Her disability was caused by the drug thalidomide, which her mother took when she was pregnant. "My interest has been in the experiences of disadvantaged persons," she said, "and looking for ways to establish a new equilibrium where people on the outside of power can get access to the inside.[24]

Sampson and her organization the Equality Effect led a team of pro bono lawyers in a successful lawsuit against the Kenyan police force for their failure to protect 160 girls between the ages of three and seventeen from being raped. The court judgment made legal history, providing justice for the 160 girls and legal protection from rape for ten million Kenyan girls. "It was about legal impunity," said Sampson. "The pharmaceuticals and governments had impunity when my mother was pregnant with me. The rapists in Kenya also had impunity because the police didn't take the defilement of girls seriously."[25] Activists and lawyers are now using the "160 Girls" judgment as a precedent for protecting girls' rights in other countries.

Sampson also chairs the Thalidomide Survivors' Task Group. They are demanding compensation from the Canadian government for its failure to determine that the drug was safe and to compensate for the fact that the life expectancy of a person exposed to thalidomide is ten to fifteen years less than that of the average person because of the wear and tear on their bodies.[26] "If it weren't for my spouse, I would've been institutionalized. I couldn't go to the bathroom, I couldn't wash my hair, I couldn't feed myself," Sampson said in an interview.[27] "As a lawyer I learned there are laws that can be used to access justice and to hold perpetrators accountable . . . laws easy to enact and hard to enforce," she said in another interview.[28] This is why the Equality Effect is now working with the law, police, and community on the root causes of sexual violence experienced by girls in Kenya by training police and sponsoring public education campaigns.

✎ Breaking Bad Barriers   RJ MITTE

Representation matters in front of and behind the screen.

Breaking Bad was a TV show with a difference. It flipped the usual premise, turning a mild-mannered chemistry teacher, Walter White, into a drug lord. Another reason the show was different was that Walt Jr., the drug lord's onscreen son, had cerebral palsy (CP). Even more unique is that RJ Mitte, the actor who portrayed Walt Jr., has cerebral palsy himself. According to Marlee Matlin, one of only two actors with a disability ever to win an Oscar, only 1 percent of the roles on the big or little screen include a character with a disability,[29] even though about 20 percent of Americans have a disability.[30] Further Matlin says only 5 percent of characters with disabilities are actually played by actors with a disability. Even fewer have a speaking role, 0.5 percent, according to a study commissioned by the Screen Actors Guild.[31] The reason for beating those odds: Vince Gilligan, the creator of Breaking Bad, wanted to honor a close college friend of his who had cerebral palsy and make the character of Walt Jr. authentic.

Since the series ended in 2013, Mitte has been working to change the representation of people with disabilities in front of and behind the screen. He described his difficulty securing new roles: "Every good role and paying role that I was going to get, I was drooling in a wheelchair. That was it."[32] Mitte doesn't mind nondisabled actors playing a disabled character. He thinks it's an opportunity for an able-bodied actor to change his or her perception of disability. However, he thinks it should go both ways. "A disabled actor should be able to audition for a nondisabled role," he said.[33] Seventy-five percent of the cast and crew of *Carol of the Bells,* a new movie he stars in, have a disability. "It's extremely important to have accurate portrayals," he explained in an interview, "I mean especially when it comes to technical things like sign language or mannerisms."[34] Recently Mitte landed a recurring role in the comedy series *Now Apocalypse*. Similar to his character in *Break-*

ing Bad, his character has CP, but it doesn't define him. His role as a sculptor and love interest does. It takes time to change your mind-set that disability is a weakness, said Mitte. "We shouldn't try to ostracize someone just by what you think they can't do but more by what you know they can do."[35]

ஃ Everything Is about Us CARLA QUALTROUGH

Nothing without us because everything is about us.

Carla Qualtrough isn't the usual glad-handing politician. She doesn't recognize people when she walks into a room or a crowd, and she can't read their name tags, which could be a big deal for someone courting votes. To compensate, she lets people know that she may not recognize them the next time they meet and asks them to take the lead and introduce themselves. Qualtrough has been visually impaired since birth. She has flourished as a medal-winning Paralympic swimmer, as a human rights lawyer, and as Canada's first minister of sport and persons with disabilities by adapting and accommodating herself to a world designed for sighted people. And that's what she wants to change.

She wants a world where everyone has an equal chance at success without the onus being on them to make adjustments or to be accommodated only after they've filed a human rights complaint. She prefers that people with disabilities use their creativity and energy on other things. "I am the exception to the rule. I am not the rule," she said in an interview.[36] Qualtrough admits that she is not the kind of person who likes to make a fuss or appear too demanding. She has learned that doing so just leaves the system as it is. She's had to retrain her own brain to expect complete accessibility and not to be apologetic about it. She learned the importance of taking a systems approach when she was a Paralympic swimmer. It helped her realize that it's possible to design a system for inclusion from the start, not after the fact. "You can't cut corners," she said. "Swimming 11 times a week, for 11 years taught me that you can't cut corners."[37] Which is why she embedded the principle of inclusion in her country's first Accessibility Act.

As a cabinet minister, Qualtrough has responsibilities that extend far beyond her disability portfolio. She sits at a cabinet table where decisions affecting all Canadians are discussed, which of course include people with disabilities. And she brings her perspective as a woman with a disability to those discussions—even to set the agenda from time to time. That's why she is suggesting a friendly amendment to "Nothing about us without us." It is "Nothing without us, because everything is about us."[38]

Did You Know . . .

One of the signers of the US Declaration of Independence was Stephen Hopkins, a man who had cerebral palsy. While signing, he said, "My hands may tremble, my heart does not."[39]

Did You Know . . .

The English writer and poet John Milton said that he had become blind writing about freedom. He wrote in the 1600s in defense of free speech, and of freedom of the press, religion, and assembly, often by candlelight and knowing he was damaging his eyes. His political ideas influenced writers such as John Locke, whose ideas laid the foundation for the American Revolution. His poem "On His Blindness" concludes with this famous line: "They also serve who only stand and wait."[40]

ॐ LESSON 10

There Is No Independence without Interdependence

By refusing to see others as truly human, we also refuse to see ourselves as truly human. By rejecting life in others, we reject life within our own being. —JEAN VANIER

What I have learned finally is that in asking for help I offer other people an opportunity for intimacy and collaboration.
—BONNIE SHERR KLEIN

I want us to see disability as sometimes (though not always) resulting in a dependency that is but one variety of a dependency that we have all experienced at some point and to which we are all vulnerable. —EVA KITTAY

ॐ What Powell River Taught Me

SOME FEELINGS SINK so deep into the heart that only loneliness can help us find them.

The flight into the coastal town of Powell River, British Columbia, was as smooth as my certainty that I would once again be helping to make life better for people with disabilities. After all, I was a recognized North American expert. The workshop audience was mixed— mostly service providers, board members, city officials, government folks—and, in a departure from the norm, there were two people who received services from the sponsoring agency. It was the usual format: a couple of hours of brainstorming the perfect world for people with disabilities, followed by my summary and an "uplifting" call to action. The suggestions were familiar: curb cuts, jobs, therapy, more money for services and staff . . . I had no trouble reducing them to manageable

143

categories. All except these two. "I want to have a big parade and give everyone balloons and flags to wave," said a middle-aged man. "I want everyone to laugh and have a good time." And, "I want to find someone to love, someone to hug goodnight, every night," said an older woman.

Those two ideas came from the two participants with disabilities. They were ignored for the rest of the day. Something about them made my flight out of town bumpy and eventually shook me out of my professional complacency. I wrestled with the memory of them for months until I finally admitted that what those two people wanted—love, intimacy, joy, and celebration—was exactly what I wanted and didn't have in my life at the time. My first marriage was disintegrating, and I was acting as if everything was fine. The realization slowly dawned on me that the only difference between me and those two souls was that they had the courage to admit it and to reach out. Who was helping whom?

The inescapable fact of life is that we are interdependent. We start life that way. Most of us will end life that way. It's the tender periods in between that we have trouble accepting or admitting. Ask any world-class athletes the secret of their success, and they will answer that it's the support of family and friends. They place it higher than talent and hard work. There is no such thing as excellence or independence without interdependence. Everything that happens in our life can be traced back to a caring relationship. Whether it's in business, politics, play, school, work, or love, we make our way in the world only because of the caring actions of others. The presence of heartbreak, personal upheaval, chronic illness, infirmity, or disability doesn't create vulnerability. Our refusal to acknowledge our dependence on the support of others does.

The denial of dependency is a personal, organizational, and societal weakness. We pretend to be who we are not. We develop a false sense of power. We allow our culture to perpetuate the myth of independence, as if it had emerged fully formed without debt or responsibility. And we rob those who are open about their vulnerability, like the two people in Powell River, of one of their greatest gifts: teaching the rest of us how to live and love with our vulnerabilities.

This lesson profiles people who understand that we are in the same leaky rowboat together. They have learned that sharing their weaknesses, mistakes, and difficulties is more nourishing to others than sharing their achievements. This lesson explores the truth about vulnerability: that this is who we are. It's what makes us human. My wish is that we create a culture that celebrates our reliance on each other, and that doesn't take those giving and receiving care for granted.

✂ Becoming Human JEAN VANIER

Love is doing ordinary things with tenderness.

Jean Vanier was born into privilege and wealth and the power that comes with it. He spent his early adult life controlling and commanding people. He was a British naval commander and professor of philosophy. In 1964, at the age of thirty-six, he left his worldly life behind and set up house in Trosly-Breuil, a small village in France, with Raphael and Phillipe, two men who had developmental disabilities. They had been living in a nearby institution. Vanier saw their beauty shining through what he described as a place of gloom and desperation. Their small stone house had no plumbing or electricity. It was as humble and ordinary as their ambition to share meals and chores and to help each other out. Their way of living soon became a destination for spiritual seekers and a place of pilgrimage for university students. It eventually inspired 150 similar communities in thirty-eight countries. These communities are called L'Arche (the ark). L'Arche communities are havens where people with and without disabilities commit to live together and to take care of each other. Vanier remained in the original L'Arche community for the rest of his life. He died in May 2019 at the age of ninety.

Vanier's thirty books and speeches describe his struggles and fears. He spent a lot of his life pretending and hiding from his own weaknesses. "Living with people with disabilities, I've touched my own brokenness, my own angers, my own powers of violence, my own capacity to hate," he told an interviewer.[1] He quoted Martin Luther King Jr., who said that unless we accept what is despicable in ourselves, we will continue to despise others. It's important to accept our imperfections, he wrote in *Seeing Beyond Depression*, because "we too have our share in wrongdoing: we have wounded our parents, our children, our husband, our wife, and our friends. When we realize this, we do not have to condemn ourselves but rather to learn to accept our own poverty and inner brokenness."[2] Vanier traveled the world reminding people that it is better to be loved than admired. "When you admire people, you put them on pedestals. When you love people, you want to be together," he said in an interview.[3]

People compare Vanier to Mother Teresa, the Dalai Lama, and Billy Graham. In 2015, he won the Templeton Prize, which at $1.7 million is worth more than the Nobel Prize. It was established by American investment banker John Templeton to celebrate entrepreneurs of the spirit. The citation described Vanier as an extraordinary man whose message of compassion for society's weakest members had the potential to change the world for the better. Vanier was never comfortable with the word *extraordinary*. His spirituality was located in the messy reality of ordinary life. He believed that the world is changed one heart at a time and that it starts with our own heart. In his book *Becoming Human*, he wrote, "Love doesn't mean doing extraordinary or heroic things. It means knowing how to do ordinary things with tenderness," he said.[4]

Vanier described himself as a pretty ordinary guy, more like a rabbit paying attention only to what was in front of him and nibbling away. And what was in front of him were two insights into how to become more human. The first is to admit your own struggles and imperfections. "I am struck," he wrote in *Community and Growth*, "by how sharing our weakness and difficulties is more nourishing to others than sharing our qualities and successes."[5] The second is to pay attention to those whom others view as weak. "The broken and the oppressed have taught me a great deal and have changed me quite radically," he wrote in *From Brokenness to Community*. "They have helped me discover that healing takes place at the bottom of the ladder, not at the top."[6]

❧ Love's Labor EVA KITTAY

The ability to love and care is as important
as the ability to think and reason.

Eva Kittay wants philosophy to become more humble and down to earth. She wants it to include the insights that come from the caring actions that most people do every day, everywhere—actions that are largely invisible and unappreciated. This is a subject close to her heart. She has been a professor of philosophy at the State University of New York at Stony Brook since 1979. And she has been caring for her daughter Sesha, who has a developmental disability, for more than fifty years. Her daughter deepened her understanding of what it means to be human, the nature of dependency, and the importance of caring relationships to keeping democracy healthy.

It took Kittay nearly thirty years to incorporate her personal experiences into her philosophical writing. It came pouring out in her essay "Not My Way, Sesha. Your Way. Slowly." Kittay believes that philosophy whitewashes disability and excludes people like her daughter from theories of personhood and human value. She believes the ability to love and care for another is as critical as the ability to think and reason, that the intellect should not rule supreme, and that the daily giving and receiving of care is what makes us human. She wants to end our fear and loathing of dependency because it is central to our existence as social creatures.[7] In her book *Love's Labor*, she argues "that there are moments when we are not 'inter' dependent. We are simply dependent and cannot reciprocate."[8]

In Love's Labor, Kittay says that a sense of justice and a sense of caring need to be cultivated together: in men, so that they have a sense of caring as deep and extensive as women's; in feminists, so that they make taking care the "most basic of women's rights"; and in the public arena, so that those who provide love's labor don't become poor and less able to get the kind of care they will need as they become older. In the area of caring, what goes around doesn't come around, she says.[9]

✎ Purple, Green, and Yellow
ROBERT MUNSCH

Supportive networks are a lifeline.

Robert Munsch is the king of children's literature, with titles like *The Paper Bag Princess*, *Mud Puddle*, and *Thomas' Snowsuit*. Children giggle along with the predicaments of his characters, particularly the adult ones. They love the snap and crackle of his words when the books are read out loud. Adults love them too, including Oprah. Her favorite children's book is *Love You Forever*. It has sold more than thirty million copies worldwide, becoming one of the best selling picture books ever. It is a memorial to Munsch and his wife Ann's two babies who were stillborn.

Despite his successes, Munsch felt a failure. A "Note to Parents" on his website explains why. "I am a storyteller," it reads. "I write books for kids, I talk to kids, and I listen to kids. But that is not all that I am. Several years ago I was diagnosed as obsessive-compulsive and manic-depressive. Those challenges have led me to make some big mistakes."[10] Munsch went public with his addiction to alcohol and cocaine in 2010. It didn't feel right not to come clean, he said, especially since he made his living teaching kids about honesty. "It made me talk about my own life the same way I talked about things in books, not sugar-coating them."[11]

Munsch was born in Pittsburgh and now lives in Guelph, Ontario. He says that his book *Purple, Green and Yellow* is about depression. In it, a girl named Brigid draws on her entire body with "super-indelible-never-come-off-till-you're-dead-and-maybe-even-later coloring markers." When Brigid washes, she becomes invisible, much to her mother's horror. "Don't worry," says Brigid, as she colors herself all over till she looks perfect. "Even better than before."[12]

Munsch told an interviewer that he too colored himself for the world, beginning when he was in grade school. He kept his struggles with depression a secret, although his mood swings were impossible to hide from his family and closest friends. For twenty years he refused to seek help and used alcohol and drugs to deal with his depression. Thanks to an ultimatum from his wife, he finally got help. He says his life is so much better now, that he is no longer suicidal. He also says that conditions like his can happen to anybody: "It doesn't matter how good you are, you can have a problem, and being open and having a support group is vital to beating it."[13]

❧ Moonbeams IAN BROWN

Love is the evolutionary advantage.

Ian Brown is a journalist and author with a reputation for serving up his emotions with unflinching honesty. He is also father to Walker, who was born with a rare genetic condition that affects only a few hundred people in the world. Walker doesn't communicate by speech and experiences profound seizures. Brown's candor is controversial. His best-selling book, *The Boy in the Moon: A Father's Journey to Understand His Extraordinary Son,* has made him a target of criticism. Some parents think that writing about his resentments, doubts, exhaustion, and questions about the meaning of his son's life should be banished or at the very least kept to himself—that it will give the wrong impression to those who know nothing about disability. They don't realize that Brown has always sorted out the challenges and changes of his life in public.

In his book, Brown described himself and his son as equals because they were both at a loss as to how to interact with each other. He interviewed scientists, philosophers, and service providers, carrying his love for Walker like a stone in his pocket and striving to understand what his son was trying to show him—a son who Brown said would never take a conventional path to success. This lack of normal expectations freed them to be themselves, he said, and "to remember who we are and what actually matters, as opposed to what is supposed to matter."[14] He realized that the world his son led him into was "almost by definition anti-establishment; a world where social orthodoxy and conventional wisdom and received opinions have very little value," and found that "that turns out to be a good vantage point."[15]

Brown discovered that every question about what was inside his son's head and heart persuaded him to look inside his own. He concluded that Walker represented a "(very small) step towards the *evolution* of a more varied and resilient ethical sense in a few members of the human species,"[16] and that his son "has few peers as a route to developing what Darwin himself in *The Descent of Man* called the evolutionary advantages of 'the social instincts . . . love, and the distinct emotion of sympathy.'"[17]

❧ The Four Walls of Her Freedom
DONNA THOMSON

Caring means letting go of control and making peace with uncertainty.

Writer Donna Thomson has many specialties. One is letting go: of her life as an actor, director, and teacher in order to care for her son Nicholas and younger daughter Natalie. And then letting go of Nicholas—to adulthood and to leaving home.

Nicholas was born with severe and complex disabilities. He is now in his thirties. One part of his story involves multiple major surgeries, living with chronic pain, spending most of his time in bed, and becoming a candidate for palliative care. The other part involves having a wicked sense of humor; graduating from high school; and maintaining *The Sports Ambassador*, a blog where the reader is invited to open a cold one and read on. Then there is his obsession with professional wrestling, particularly Stone Cold Steve Austin, and starting a business on eBay.

Thomson's husband, Jim Wright, now retired, was one of Canada's top diplomats, with postings in Washington, Moscow, and London. His final posting was as Canada's high commissioner to the UK, which meant that Jim and Donna hosted the queen, presidents, and prime ministers. Through it all, Donna and Nick were glued at the hip.

She named her first book *The Four Walls of My Freedom* after a quote by the American philosopher Thomas Merton, who found his freedom only after entering a monastery in Kentucky. Thomson found similar enlightenment in the social isolation she experienced as a caregiver. Mothering a child with medical needs is a very public but lonely endeavor, she said in an interview. "It is a strange paradox that in order to be free, the mother of a child with severe disabilities in our society has to relinquish the choosing self."[18] Locating the extraordinary in the ordinary made her happy. Tiny everyday actions became a form of meditation, even peeling potatoes. She realized, "Freedom isn't an exertion of power but an exercise of restraint."[19]

That doesn't mean it was easy. Being responsible for a loved one who was so fragile felt like a prison at times. "There were days that I felt furious and impotent with my inability to make personal choices or to act spontaneously . . . ever," she wrote.[20] "But I was always seduced again into laughter and optimism by the smell of my children's hair, the touch of their fingers on my arm, or the whispers of their secrets in my ear."[21]

When it came time for Nicholas to leave home, she had to let go of her caregiver identity. She said she was getting too old to remain as the "CEO of the Nicholas Wright Corporation" anyway. She no longer had the strength to reposition her son in his wheelchair. She's learned to trust those who are now caring for Nick. "I learned the hard way that letting go of control and making peace with uncertainty is the key to feeling relaxed and even happy most of the time," she wrote on her popular blog, *The Caregivers' Living Room*.[22]

✃ The Untouchables PHILIPPE POZZO DI BORGO AND ABDEL SELLOU

Weakness is a treasure worth discovering.

Driss is handsome, cool, and cocky. The world is his oyster. Except that he is just out of prison and needs money. He shows up for a job interview, not to get the job but to get another letter of rejection that will allow him to keep receiving welfare benefits. Instead he gets the job. No one could be less interested or qualified. His new employer is Philippe. Philippe broke his neck in a paragliding accident. He is wealthy and can hire anyone he wants. Driss is the only candidate who doesn't treat him with pity. Thus begins *The Intouchables*, also known as *The Untouchables*, the most successful French film ever made.

Driss's caregiving methods are unconventional. He assumes that Philippe will be interested in what he is interested in: women, fast cars, boogeying. There are car chases, gang wars, and tenderness. Both men are lonely in their own way. Both are treated as untouchable—

one because of his disability, the other because of his race and socio-economic status.

The film was inspired by the true story of Philippe Pozzo di Borgo and his French-Algerian caregiver, Abdel Sellou. Pozzo di Borgo's book is titled *A Second Wind: A Memoir*. Three years after his accident, his wife, Béatrice, died of cancer. "Weakness is not a handicap," he said in an interview, "but a treasure that others still have to discover."[23] Pozzo di Borgo doesn't distinguish between those who have a disability and those who don't. "All people are dependent on each other," he said. "They need to take better care of each other. . . . We're not always beautiful, athletic, immortal. We are—the older we become—fragile."[24]

His real-life attendant Abdel Sellou also wrote a book, *You Changed My Life*. He said in an interview that he wasn't particularly endearing when he first met Pozzo di Borgo. "I used to just be concerned with myself," he said. "I was a lone wolf, egotistical and unscrupulous."[25] He wrote in his book that he hadn't done that much for Pozzo di Borgo, "at least not as much as he did for me."[26] Pozzo di Borgo views it differently. "He was unbearable, vain, proud, brutal, inconsistent, human. Without him, I would have rotted to death. . . . He was my guardian devil."[27]

✆ Poem for Michael KIRSTEEN MAIN

Friendship is silent communion.

Kirsteen Main is a Canadian poet who composes using an alphabet board, a device that enables her to gesture in the direction of the letter she has chosen. "Not being able to speak is not the same as not having anything to say," Main wrote in the opening to *Dear Butterfly*, her first collection of poetry and painting.[28] The following poem was written to honor her lifelong friendship with Michael Wittman.

To Michael

You are the friend
Everyone deserves.
You are a friend I respect and admire.
With you I can be exactly
Who I am.
There is no need to
Feel invisible.
You understand in a way
No one else can.
Silent communication comforts me,
Gives strength to our lives, adds hope for our future.[29]

❦ There Is No Independence without Interdependence BONNIE SHERR KLEIN

Asking for help gives people an opportunity to be their most human.

Bonnie Sherr Klein is an award-winning documentary filmmaker. She was one of the first directors in Studio D, the feminist unit at the National Film Board (NFB) of Canada. One of the NFB's most commonly screened films is *Not a Love Story*, the first documentary about pornography from a woman's point of view. Filmmaking and feminism defined her identity into her forties, until a summer weekend at the family's Vermont cabin. That's where the first of her two major strokes happened. She would have died from the second one had it not been for the tenacity of her doctor husband, Michael Klein. After an exhaustive search, he found a surgeon willing to perform a delicate eight-hour operation that saved her life. Her book, *Slow Dance: A Story of Stroke, Love, and Disability*, recounts the story of her recovery from paralysis, being unable to speak and reliant on a respirator. After many years of rehabilitation and meeting other people with disabilities, she settled into her new identity as a woman with a disability.

Nowadays Klein gets around in a motorized scooter that she calls Gladys, named after a suffragette who learned how to ride a bicycle later in life. She wrote, "Before my stroke, I had a mistaken notion that feminism meant 'independence'; the unspoken corollary was that dependence on others is shameful. What I've learned finally is that in asking for help I offer other people an opportunity for intimacy and collaboration. Whether I'm asking for me personally or for disabled people generally, I give them the opportunity to be their most human. In Judaism, we call this gift a mitzvah."[30]

One of the many people who were changed by the experience of caring was Klein's daughter Naomi. Naomi Klein is the author of *No Logo* and *This Changes Everything*. She was seventeen at the time of her mother's strokes and about to enter university. Instead, she took time off to help the family care for her mother. It was a formative moment. She saw how trauma could bring out the best in people. It influenced her writing of *The Shock Doctrine*. "In a shocked state, with our understanding of the world badly shaken, a great many of us can become childlike and passive," she told an interviewer, "and overly trusting of people who are only too happy to abuse that trust."[31] Or, as she learned from her family's experience, "we can evolve and grow up in a crisis, and set aside all kinds of bullshit—fast."[32] The *New Yorker* once described Naomi Klein as the most influential figure on the American left. She wrote in an essay for the *Nation* that "'I care about you' . . . is a deeply radical statement."[33]

At the end of *Slow Dance*, Bonnie Klein wrote that she knew she could live well without the role or title of filmmaker. She wondered whether she would ever make another film. Eight years later she did. She directed *Shameless: The ART of Disability*, which profiles five artists who have a disability. She is one of them. The film confronts with gentle humor the images that the public has about disability, including the ones that Klein used to have, which is one of the reasons why she made the film. She admits in the film that at first she didn't want to be identified as someone who had a disability, that she couldn't stand to walk by a mirror and see herself. "Art reveals the best and worst parts of ourselves to each other," she says. "It is shameless. The people I know now because of my stroke have enriched my life and are my teachers and mentors. They're fellow travelers and they're artists."[34]

ᖆ CONCLUSION

Life Comes from Life

Having a disability means that we are all the same. There is no difference, and that is an amazing and beautiful thing
—LIZ ETMANSKI

THE ULTIMATE LESSON taught by the people you have just read about is that life comes from life.

It comes from life in every shape, size, and background. Complex lives. Messy lives. Struggling lives. Determined lives. Funny lives. Mysterious lives. Sensual lives. Beautiful lives. Sacred lives.

It doesn't come from machines, technology, techniques, and touch-ups. Nor from artificial intelligence and artificial limbs. Nor from quick fixes and miracle cures. Nor from positive mind-sets and exceptional heroes. These can be useful, but not as much as we have been seduced to believe. And certainly not in isolation.

A thriving life must be accompanied by a nurturing environment that includes family and friends who care about you and a society that cares about you too—cares enough to allocate resources, provide opportunities, and expand justice so that you can live life to the fullest.

Disability is emblematic of the times we live in. Of living with despair. Of struggling to get by. Of making do without recognition and appreciation. Of changing the circumstances of our lives by returning to the basic ingredient of democracy: doing things together.

There is no such thing as the disability world and the "rest of us" world. And we can't afford for there to be one. There is only one world. If we are going to preserve it, we have to make it a place where people are enlarged, not threatened, by difference. Where as many people as possible are moving in the same direction. Where we transcend our partisan and ideological beliefs and recognize, indeed rely on, what we have in common: our dependence on each other.

Of all the conditions that bind us together, the experience of disability is the most universal and therefore the most unifying. It's not just the fact that it touches the majority of people on the planet. It's that it offers us an alternative to the lone-actor, epic-hero story that abounds. It gives us a story that celebrates our deep connections to each other and to the earth—a story that reminds us that none of us get where we are going on our own and that success doesn't come from rising above but by rising with.

We are not separate. Although we are different, we don't have to be alone. We all breathe life, live life, love life, give life, leave life. And we inhabit this fragile, beautiful, and living planet together. The power of disability is the power of that life.

Notes

❧ Introduction: **The Disability Advantage**

1. Rich Donovan, *Return on Disability: Translate Different into Value*, May 1, 2016, 2, http://www.rod-group.com/sites/default/files/2016%20Annual%20 Report%20-%20The%20Global%20Economics%20of%20Disability.pdf.

2. Tara Bitran, "USC Disability Panel Emphasizes Initiative, Tenacity in Face of Bias in Hollywood," *Variety*, May 2, 2018, https://variety.com/2018/artisans /news/usc-disability-good-doctor-1202794809/ (accessed June 28, 2019).

3. Ashley Chappo, "The Stunning Story of the Woman Who Is the World's Most Popular Artist," Observer, https://observer.com/2015/04/the-stunning -story-of-the-woman-who-is-the-worlds-most-popular-artist/ (accessed March 4, 2019).

4. Suyin Haynes, "The Story Behind TIME's Greta Thunberg Cover," *Time*, http://time.com/collection-post/5588274/greta-thunberg-time-cover-portrait/ (accessed May 31, 2019).

❧ A Word about Words

1. For more details, see the US Census or Statistics Canada.

2. @GHMansfield, April 21, 2019.

3. Institute for the Study of the Neurologically Typical, http://erikengdahl.se /autism/isnt/index.html.

❧ Lesson 1: **If It Ain't Broke, Don't Fix It**

What Gord Walker Taught Me

1. In memory of Gordon Walker (1953–2011).

Body Politics Catherine Frazee

2. Catherine Frazee, "Body Politics," *Saturday Night*, September 2, 2000.

Brilliant Imperfection Eli Clare

3. CBC Radio, "'My cerebral palsy isn't a problem to be cured,' says writer Eli Clare," "Tapestry," https://www.cbc.ca/radio/tapestry/rethinking-disability -1.4726131/my-cerebral-palsy-isn-t-a-problem-to-be-cured-says-writer-eli-clare -1.4726305 (accessed November 1, 2018).

4. CBC Radio, "'My cerebral palsy isn't a problem to be cured,' says writer Eli Clare."

5. CBC Radio.

6. Eli Clare, *Brilliant Imperfection: Grappling with Cure* (Durham, NC: Duke University Press, 2017).

7. Eli Clare, "Body Shame, Body Pride: Lessons from the Disability Rights Movement," *Live Journal*, April 2, 2007, https://pitbull-poet.livejournal.com /21560.html (accessed November 6, 2018).

8. Clare, "Body Shame, Body Pride."

The Gift Judith Snow

9. Judith Snow, recollection at a personal appearance, September 1985.

10. Judith Snow, personal conversation with the author, June 1989.

11. *Great Questions: Writings of Judith Snow* (Toronto, Canada: Inclusion Press, 2016), https://inclusion.com/product/great-questions-writings-of-judith -snow-ebook/.

A Brief History of Imperfection Dr. Stephen Hawking

12. *Into the Universe with Stephen Hawking*, miniseries, Discovery Channel, 2010.

13. Jessica Roy, "Erasing Stephen Hawking's disability erases an important part of who he was," *Los Angeles Times*, March 16, 2018, https://www.latimes .com/science/sciencenow/la-sci-sn-stephen-hawking-disability-rights-20180316 -story.html.

14. Alan Lightman and Roberta Brawer, *Origins: The Lives and Worlds of Modern Cosmologists* (Cambridge, MA: Harvard University Press, 1990).

15. "Remember to look up at the stars: The best Stephen Hawking quotes," *Guardian*, https://www.theguardian.com/science/2018/mar/14/best-stephen -hawking-quotes-quotations (accessed October 3, 2018).

If It Ain't Broke, Don't Fix It The Schappell Twins

16. Dulcie Pearce, "We have normal lives," *Sun*, September 12, 2011, https://www.thesun.co.uk/archives/news/776690/we-have-normal-lives/ (accessed May 4, 2017).

17. Pearce, "We have normal lives."

18. Pearce.

19. Natalie Angier, "Joined for Life, and Living Life to the Full," *New York Times*, December 23, 1997, https://www.nytimes.com/1997/12/23/science/joined-for-life-and-living-life-to-the-full.html (accessed May 4, 2017).

20. *Face to Face: The Story of the Schappell Twins*, A&E Home Video, 2002.

Hidden Wholeness Parker Palmer

21. Center for Courage & Renewal, http://www.couragerenewal.org/parker/.

22. Zoe Mackey, "The View From the Brink: Parker Palmer on Grace, Gravity, and Getting Old," BK Connection, June 25, 2018, https://ideas.bkconnection.com/the-view-from-the-brink-parker-palmer-on-grace-gravity-and-getting-old (accessed June 26, 2018).

23. Alicia Von Stamwitz, "If Only We Would Listen," *Sun*, November 2012, https://thesunmagazine.org/issues/443/if-only-we-would-listen (accessed July 31, 2018).

24. Parker J. Palmer, "Welcome to the Human Race," *Daily Good*, http://www.dailygood.org/story/1762/welcome-to-the-human-race/ (accessed July 31, 2018).

25. Parker J. Palmer, *A Hidden Wholeness: The Journey Toward an Undivided Life* (San Francisco, CA: Jossey-Bass, 2004).

26. Palmer, "Welcome to the Human Race."

27. Von Stamwitz, "If Only We Would Listen."

28. Von Stamwitz.

29. Parker J. Palmer, *Let Your Life Speak: Listening for the Voice of Vocation* (San Francisco, CA: Jossey-Bass, 1999).

Humanity Passport Naoki Higashida with David Mitchell

30. Naoki Higashida, *Fall Down 7 Times Get Up 8: A Young Man's Voice from the Silence of Autism* (New York: Knopf, 2017).

31. David Mitchell, "David Mitchell: Learning to live with my son's autism," *Guardian*, June 29, 2013, https://www.theguardian.com/society/2013/jun/29/david-mitchell-my-sons-autism?CMP=twt_fbo (accessed June 23, 2018).

32. Mike Doherty, "David Mitchell on translating—and learning from— Naoki Higashida," *Maclean's*, July 13, 2017, https://www.macleans.ca/society /david-mitchell-on-translating-and-learning-from-naoki-higashida/ (accessed July 14, 2017).

33. Nate Hopper, "My Autism Allows Me to See the World in a Different Way," *Time*, July 13, 2017, https://time.com/4856602/autism-nonverbal-book -naoki-higashida/.

34. Naoki Higashida, *The Reason I Jump: The Inner Voice of a Thirteen-Year-Old Boy with Autism* (Toronto, Canada: Vintage Canada, 2016).

35. Higashida, *The Reason I Jump*.

A Culture with No Boundaries Carey, Shelly, and Zoe Elverum

36. CBC Radio, "An unusual family finds joy, connection and love in a remote Inuit community," "The Sunday Edition," September 10, 2017, https:// www.cbc.ca/radio/thesundayedition/the-sunday-edition-september-10-2017-1 .4280530/an-unusual-family-finds-joy-connection-and-love-in-a-remote-inuit -community-1.4280762 (accessed September 18, 2017).

37. Jennifer Kingsley, "Meet the Elverums," Meet the North, September 17, 2017, https://www.meetthenorth.org/2017/09/meet-the-elverums/ (accessed September 18, 2017).

38. Kingsley, "Meet the Elverums."

39. Kingsley.

40. Kingsley.

℘ Lesson 2: **Funny Things Happen on the Way to the Future**

What David Roche Taught Me

1. David Roche, *The Church of 80% Sincerity* (New York: Penguin, 2012).

2. David Roche, "The Metaphor of Facial Difference," Well of Light, https:// www.welloflight.com/the-metaphor-of-facial-difference.html (accessed January 15, 2018).

3. David Roche, recollection in a personal appearance, January 27, 2014.

Funny Things Happen on the Way to the Future Michael J. Fox

4. Brian D. Johnson, "Michael J. Fox: Back with a future," *Maclean's*, October 6, 2013, *https://www.macleans.ca/culture/back-with-a-future/* (accessed September 26, 2018).

5. Brian Hiatt, "Michael J. Fox: The Toughest Man on TV," *Rolling Stone*, September 26, 2013, https://www.rollingstone.com/tv/tv-news/michael-j-fox-the-toughest-man-on-tv-195820/ (accessed September 26, 2018).

6. Ian Youngs, "Jodie Foster and Michael J. Fox lead anti-trump protest," BBC, February 25, 2017, https://www.bbc.com/news/entertainment-arts-39088450 (accessed September 26, 2018).

7. Marlo Thomas, "The Givers: What Inspires Michael J. Fox? A Very Personal Interview," HuffPost, April 5, 2012, https://www.huffpost.com/entry/michael-j-fox-interview_b_1402876.

8. Andrew Corsello, "The Kid Is Alright," *AARP* magazine, March 22, 2017, https://www.aarp.org/entertainment/style-trends/info-2017/michael-j-fox-aarp-magazine.html.

Laughing Matters Maysoon Zayid

9. Maysoon Zayid, "I Got 99 Problems . . . Palsy Is Just One," TED Talk, December 2013.

10. Zayid, "I Got 99 Problems . . . Palsy Is Just One."

11. Xiaorong Chen, "We are not making history, we are changing the story," UNESCO Courier, https://en.unesco.org/courier/lrsl-lrqmy/maysoon-zayid-we-are-not-making-history-we-are-changing-story (accessed June 29, 2019).

12. Bligh Voth, "Maysoon," Nasty Women of New York, https://www.nastywomenofnewyork.com/nwny-1/2018/4/13/maysoon (accessed June 29, 2019).

13. Ellen McGirt, "Can This Disabled, Muslim, Female Comic Save the RNC? She Sure Is Trying," *Fortune*, July 20, 2016, http://fortune.com/2016/07/20/maysoon-zavid-rnc-muslim-comic/ (accessed June 29, 2019).

14. McGirt, "Can This Disabled, Muslim, Female Comic Save the RNC?"

15. Zayid, "I Got 99 Problems . . . Palsy Is Just One."

If at Birth You Don't Succeed Zach Anner

16. Zach Anner, *If at Birth You Don't Succeed: My Adventures with Disaster and Destiny* (New York: Henry Holt & Co., 2016).

17. Zach Anner, "Top 10 Things I Wish People Knew about Cerebral Palsy," YouTube, September 17, 2016, https://www.youtube.com/watch?v=w-Sh8Zu GbMI (accessed June 2, 2019).

18. Zach Anner, "Pullups and Pick-me-ups—Workout Wednesday," YouTube, Zach Anner, https://www.youtube.com/watch?v=JqEQ4SSdZAs&list=PLKid_CN BQaE7a_lDb6HCRJe1eSlRrQ9KW (accessed June 2, 2019).

19. @Zachanner.

Changing the World One Laugh at a Time Nidhi Goyal

20. Nidhi Goyal, "Changing the World One Laugh at a Time," Comedy for Disability Rights, TEDxHRCollege, April 13, 2018, https://www.youtube.com /watch?v=bNdVlwFptfU (accessed April 10, 2019).

21. Nidhi Goyal, "In the words of Nidhi Goyal: 'These spaces are for everyone,'" UN Women, June 13, 2018, http://www.unwomen.org/en/news/stories /2018/6/in-the-words-of-nidhi-goyal (accessed April 10, 2019).

22. Centre for Social Research, "Gender in Indian Standup Comedy—Nidhi Goyal," Gender Matters, January 23, 2018, http://gendermatters.in/2018/01 /nidhi-goyal-gender-in-indian-standup-comedy/.

23. Goyal, "Changing the World One Laugh at a Time."

24. Goyal.

25. UN India, "8 Women, 8 Incredible Stories," May 11, 2017, https:// un-india.exposure.co/8-women-8-incredible-stories?embed=true (accessed April 10, 2019).

Don't Worry, He Won't Get Far on Foot John Callahan

26. Bruce Weber, "John Callahan, Cartoonist, Dies at 59," *New York Times*, July 28, 2010, https://www.nytimes.com/2010/07/28/arts/design/28callahan.html accessed June 29, 2019).

27. Robert Chalmers, "Prophet of bad taste: John Callahan was a comic genius who left no taboo unbroken," August 13, 2010, Independent, https:// www.independent.co.uk/arts-entertainment/comedy/features/prophet-of-bad -taste-john-callahan-was-a-comic-genius-who-left-no-taboo-unbroken-2051210 .html (accessed June 29, 2019).

Get Down Moves Lauren Potter

28. *Fandom*, "Lauren Potter," https://glee.fandom.com/wiki/Lauren_Potter (accessed February 28, 2018).

29. *Fandom*, "Lauren Potter."

30. Lauren Potter, "I'm Taking a Stand to Make My Difference in the World," HuffPost, June 2, 2014, https://www.huffpost.com/entry/im-taking-a-stand-to -make_b_5431373 (accessed February 28, 2018).

31. Potter, "I'm Taking a Stand to Make My Difference in the World."

32. Caitlin Gallagher, "Glee's Lauren Potter Has a Message for Hollywood on Hiring People with Down Syndrome: 'You Won't Be Disappointed,'" Popsugar, October 19, 2018, https://www.popsugar.com/smart-living/Lauren

-PotterInterview-About-Acting-Down-Syndrome-45290908 (accessed February 28, 2019).

Smart Ass Empire Mike Ervin

33. Mike Ervin, "The Birth of a Smart Ass Empire," *Smart Ass Cripple*, http:// smartasscripple.blogspot.com/2010/10/birth-of-smart-ass-empire.html (accessed December 8, 2018).

34. Ervin, "The Birth of a Smart Ass Empire."

35. Roger Ebert, "This Cripple is a Smart Ass," *Roger Ebert's Journal*, https:// www.rogerebert.com/rogers-journal/this-cripple-is-a-smart-ass (accessed December 8, 2018).

36. Mike Ervin, "Rent-A-Cripple," *Smart Ass Cripple*, http://smartasscripple .blogspot.com/2012/01/rent-cripple.html (accessed December 8, 2018).

Funny, You Don't Look Crazy Victoria Maxwell

37. Karen Barrow, "A Patient Takes the Stage," *New York Times*, https:// www.nytimes.com/interactive/2017/well/patient-voices-bipolar.html#victoria (accessed May 30, 2019).

38. Victoria Maxwell, "A Brief History of a Lucky Woman," *Psychology Today*, February 12, 2019, https://www.psychologytoday.com/ca/blog/crazy-life/201902 /brief-history-lucky-woman (accessed May 30, 2019).

39. Victoria Maxwell, "Rules for Making Fun of Mental Illness," *Psychology Today*, February 21, 2018, https://www.psychologytoday.com/us/blog/crazy-life /201802/rules-making-fun-mental-illness (accessed May 30, 2019).

40. Maxwell, "Rules for Making Fun of Mental Illness" (used with permission).

Did You Know . . .

41. Joelle Smith, "Estimated 98% of World's Banking Leaders Pre-Collapse Are Non-Autistic," Evil Autie, April 5, 2013, https://evilautie.org/2013/04/05 /estimated-98-of-worlds-banking-leaders-pre-collapse-are-non-autistic/?fbclid =IwAR0EDQ6PUuWJHPDQTbiMBsb4NW84gJZ0v63c2Yh- (accessed June 29, 2019).

42. Susan Devaney, "Nanette's Hannah Gadsby reveals how autism diagnosis transformed her," Stylist, https://www.stylist.co.uk/people/nanette-hannah -gadsby-autism-tv-comedy-netflix/218114 (accessed June 29, 2019).

✑ Lesson 3: **Label Jars, Not People**

What Cradle Heaven Taught Me

1. Facility name and circumstances have been changed.

The Mismeasure of Man Stephen Jay Gould

2. Henry Herbert Goddard, *The Kallikak Family: A Study in the Heredity of Feeble-Mindedness* (London, England: Forgotten Books, 2012; originally published in 1913).

3. Stephen Jay Gould, *The Mismeasure of Man* (New York: W. W. Norton, 1996).

4. Stephen Jay Gould, *Full House: The Spread of Excellence from Plato to Darwin* (Cambridge, MA: Belknap Press, 2011).

5. Daniel S. Levy and Stephen Jay Gould, "Evolution, Extinction and the Movies," *Time*, May 14, 1990.

The Power of Not Fitting In Temple Grandin

6. Temple Grandin, *Temple Grandin's Guide to Working with Farm Animals: Safe, Humane Livestock Handling Practices for the Small Farm* (North Adams, MA: Storey Publishing, 2017).

7. Neal Conan, "Temple Grandin: A Life Devoted to Animals," NPR, January 27, 2010, https://www.npr.org/templates/story/story.php?storyId=123028845 (accessed May 3, 2019).

8. Temple Grandin, "The World Needs All Kinds of Minds," TED Talk.

Dethroning Stereotypes Peter Dinklage

9. James Hibberd, "Peter Dinklage talks 'Game of Thrones' at Comic-Con," *Entertainment*, July 21, 2011, https://ew.com/article/2011/07/21/peter-dinklage-game-of-thrones/ (accessed June 1, 2018).

10. Sarah Luoma, "Peter Dinklage on His First Animated Movie, 'Ice Age 4': "I felt like I was doing everything wrong," *Daily Actor*, July 18, 2012, https://www.dailyactor.com/film/peter-dinklage-ice-age-4/ (accessed June 1, 2018).

11. Gael Fashingbauer, "George R. R. Martin tells voters how to get rid of a bad king," CNET, https://www.cnet.com/news/george-r-r-martin-tells-voters-how-to-get-rid-of-a-bad-king/ (accessed June 2, 2018).

12. Eric Spitznagel, "Peter Dinklage's Porn Name Is, Not Surprisingly, Peter Dinklage," *Vanity Fair*, January 20, 2011, https://www.vanityfair.com/culture/2011

/01/peter-dinklages-porn-name-is-not-surprisingly-peter-dinklage (accessed June 2, 2018).

Identity Complications Cristina Hartmann

13. Cristina Hartmann, "About," https://cristinahartmann.com/about (accessed February 13, 2019).

14. Cristina Hartmann, "Reading Between the Lines I Couldn't See," Medium, November 2, 2018, https://medium.com/s/story/the-library-my-savior -d853f2b8ec4f (accessed February 13, 2019).

15. Hartmann, "Reading Between the Lines I Couldn't See."

16. Cristina Hartmann, "The Complications of Growing Up Bionic," Medium, February 11, 2018, https://medium.com/s/for-the-record/neither-a -miracle-nor-a-tragedy-the-complications-of-growing-up-bionic-4c78a4c7d722.

17. Hartmann, "Reading Between the Lines I Couldn't See."

The R-Word Timothy Shriver

18. Manuel Roig-Franzia, "Special O chair urges respect for intellectually disabled," *Daily Herald*, March 28, 2010, https://www.heraldextra.com/lifestyles /special-olympics-chair-urges-respect-for-intellectually-disabled/article_a07dfe13 -7f0b-57a7-b941-79d08e618a67.html (accessed June 14, 2019).

19. Roig-Franzia, "Special O chair urges respect for intellectually disabled."

20. Timothy Shriver, "The bigotry behind the word 'retard,'" *Washington Post*, February 15, 2010, http://www.washingtonpost.com/wp-dyn/content/article /2010/02/14/AR2010021402893.html (accessed June 14, 2019).

21. Shriver, "The bigotry behind the word 'retard.'"

22. Timothy Shriver, "Why Tropic Thunder shouldn't be seen," CNN, August 13, 2008, http://www.cnn.com/2008/SHOWBIZ/Movies/08/12/shriver.thunder/ (accessed June 14, 2019).

Breaking the Silence Allie Cashel

23. Amanda Crommett Photography, "Suffering the Silence: Portraits of Chronic Illness," Suffering the Silence, https://www.sufferingthesilence.com /portraits-of-chronic-illness (accessed May 2, 2019).

24. Anna Gragert, "Powerful Portraits of People Revealing Their Invisible Illnesses," My Modern Met, September 1, 2015, https://mymodernmet.com /cashel-lupinacci-suffering-the-silence/ (accessed May 2, 2019).

25. Mary Beth Pfeiffer, *Lyme: The First Epidemic of Climate Change* (Washington, DC: Island Press, 2018).

26. Allie Cashel, "Becoming Visible," North Atlantic Books, May 18, 2016, https://www.northatlanticbooks.com/blog/becoming-visible/ (accessed May 2, 2019).

Label Jars, Not People Edith Sheffer

27. CBC Radio, "A Nazi in all but name: Author argues Asperger's syndrome should be renamed," "The Current," August 13, 2018, http://www.cbc.ca/radio /thecurrent/the-current-for-august-14-2018-1.4783610/a-nazi-in-all-but-name -author-argues-asperger-s-syndrome-should-be-renamed-1.4783614 (accessed September 5, 2018).

28. Edith Sheffer, *Asperger's Children: The Origins of Autism in Nazi Vienna* (New York: W. W. Norton, 2018).

29. Sheffer, *Asperger's Children*.

30. CBC, "A Nazi in all but name."

31. Sheffer, *Asperger's Children*.

Branding Disability Albert Lasker

32. Terry O'Reilly, "The Most Interesting Adman in the World: The Story of Albert Lasker," CBC Radio, "Under the Influence," August 31, 2017, https://www .cbc.ca/radio/undertheinfluence/summer-series-the-most-interesting-adman-in -the-world-the-story-of-albert-lasker-1.4120833 (accessed March 2, 2019).

33. O'Reilly, "The Most Interesting Adman in the World."

34. Brittney McNamara, "Barbie Is Now in a Wheelchair and Has a Pros-thetic Leg," *Teen Vogue*, February 11, 2019, https://www.teenvogue.com/story /barbie-wheelchair-prosthetic-leg? (accessed June 3, 2019).

35. Anna Malec, "National Geographic's new photo campaign highlights people with Down syndrome," Aleteia, November 23, 2018, https://aleteia.org /2018/11/23/national-geographics-new-photo-campaign-highlights-people-with -down-syndrome/ (accessed June 3, 2019).

36. Terri Peters, "The first Gerber baby with Down syndrome will steal your heart," *Today*, February 7, 2018, https://www.today.com/parents/2018-gerber -baby-first-gerber-baby-down-syndrome-t122258 (accessed June 3, 2019).

✆ Lesson 4: **There Ain't No Cure for Love**

What Phil and Wendy Allen Taught Me

1. In memory of Phil Allen (1927–2017).

Hot, Wet, and Shaking Kaleigh Trace

2. Kaleigh Trace, "Kaleigh Trace—I Don't Feel Bad about This At All," https://vimeo.com/49564647.

3. CBC Radio, "Sex educator shares her path to radical self-acceptance," "Tapestry," July 29, 2018, https://www.cbc.ca/radio/tapestry/rethinking-disability -1.4726131/sex-educator-shares-her-path-to-radical-self-acceptance-1.4726329 (accessed October 4, 2019).

4. CBC Radio, "Sex educator shares her path to radical self-acceptance."

5. Invisible Publishing, *Hot, Wet, and Shaking: How I Learned to Talk About Sex*, https://invisiblepublishing.com/product/hot-wet-and-shaking/.

6. "Real Sex Advice from Kaleigh Trace," *Sex with Dr. Jess*, November 7, 2017, https://www.sexwithdrjess.com/2017/11/real-sex-advice-from-kaleigh-trace/ (accessed October 4, 2019).

There Ain't No Cure for Love Leonard Cohen

7. Mireille Silcott, "A Happy Man," *Saturday Night*, September 15, 2001, http://www.webheights.net/10newsongs/press/satnite.htm (accessed April 8, 2018).

8. Silcott, "A Happy Man."

9. David Remnick, "Leonard Cohen Makes It Darker," *New Yorker*, October 10, 2016, https://www.newyorker.com/magazine/2016/10/17/leonard-cohen -makes-it-darker (accessed April 8, 2018).

10. LeonardCohenForums, "Ten years . . . ," https://www.leonardcohenforum .com/viewtopic.php?t=15430 (accessed January 7, 2018).

11. Silcott, "A Happy Man."

12. Soutik Biswas, "When the light got in for Leonard Cohen," BBC News, November 16, 2016, https://www.bbc.com/news/world-asia-india-37971848 (accessed April 9, 2018).

Love at Second Sight Marlena Blavin

13. Paul Liberatore, "Facing challenges with love," *Marin Independent Journal*, March 4, 2008, https://www.marinij.com/2008/03/04/facing-challenges-with -love/ (accessed April 17, 2019).

14. "Love at Second Sight," interview, Vimeo, https://vimeo.com/65760126 (accessed April 17, 2019).

15. "Love at Second Sight," Vimeo.

16. Love at Second Sight, https://www.loveatsecondsight.org/.

17. Liberatore, "Facing challenges with love."

18. Nic Askew, SoulBiographies, "The Second Glance," http://nicaskew.com /collection/the-second-glance/ (accessed June 25, 2017).

Sex and the Gimpy Girl Nancy Mairs

19. Nancy Mairs, "Sex and the Gimpy Girl," *River Teeth* 10, no. 1–2 (Fall 2008/Spring 2009).

20. Nancy Mairs, *Waist-High in the World: A Life Among the Nondisabled* (Boston, MA: Beacon Press, 1997).

21. Mairs, *Waist-High in the World*

22. Mairs.

23. Nancy Mairs, *Carnal Acts: Essays* (New York: Perennial, 1991).

Crossing Half of China to Sleep with You Yu Xiuhua

24. Yu Xiuhua, "Two Poems," *World Literature Today*, https://www.world literaturetoday.org/2018/july/two-poems-yu-xiuhua (accessed November 15, 2018).

25. Xu Xiao, "Two Poets' War of Words Shows China's Yawning Generation Gap," Sixth Tone, February 8, 2018, http://www.sixthtone.com/news/1001688 /two-poets-war-of-words-shows-chinas-yawning-generation-gap# (accessed November 15, 2018).

26. Kiki Zhao, "A Chinese Poet's Unusual Path From Isolated Farm Life to Celebrity," *New York Times*, August 18, 2017, https://www.nytimes.com/2017/08 /18/world/asia/china-poet-yu-xiuhua.html (accessed November 15, 2018).

27. Jennifer Robinson, *POV: Still Tomorrow*, KPBS, July 24, 2018, https:// www.kpbs.org/news/2018/jul/24/pov-still-tomorrow/ (accessed November 16, 2018).

Fifty Shades of Scarlet Mik Scarlet

28. Mik Scarlet, "The man taught to have sex by lesbians," BBC News, https://www.bbc.com/news/disability-39351352 (accessed May 6, 2019).

29. Mik Scarlet and Emily Yates, *Welcome to the Love Lounge at Enhance the UK*, Real Talk, http://real-talk.org/the-love-lounge-a-web-based-advice-forum-on -sex-love-and-disability/ (accessed August 12, 2018).

30. *Scope*, "Scope's Romance Classics: Mik Scarlet Has a One Track Mind," February 11, 2016, https://blog.scope.org.uk/2016/02/11/scopes-romance-classics -mik-scarlet-has-a-one-track-mind/ (accessed August 12, 2018).

31. Katharine Quarmby, "What Disabled People Can Teach Us About Sex— and Why We Should Listen," Gizmodo, March 17, 2015, https://io9.gizmodo

.com/what-disabled-people-can-teach-us-about-sex-and-why-w-1691916261 (accessed August 12, 2018).

32. Quarmby, "What Disabled People Can Teach Us About Sex."

Things Disabled People Know about Parenting Ing Wong-Ward

33. Ing Wong-Ward, Twitter, January 20, 2019, https://twitter.com /ingwongward/status/1087186892037197824.

34. Disability Visibility Project, "DVP Interview: Ing Wong-Ward and Alice Wong," December 1, 2018, https://disabilityvisibilityproject.com/2018/12/01 /dvp-interview-ing-wong-ward-and-alice-wong/ (accessed January 25, 2019).

35. Anna Maria Tremonti, "'A compromised life is worth living': Why Ing Wong-Ward won't choose medically assisted death," CBC Radio, "The Current," May 3, 2018, https://www.cbc.ca/radio/thecurrent/the-current-for-may-3-2018 -1.4645398/a-compromised-life-is-worth-living-why-ing-wong-ward-won-t -choose-medically-assisted-death-1.4645437 (accessed January 25, 2019).

In Sickness and in Health Ben Mattlin

36. Ben Mattlin, *In Sickness and in Health: Love, Disability, and a Quest to Understand the Perils and Pleasures of Interabled Romance* (Boston, MA: Beacon Press, 2018).

37. Lisa Mullins, "Why a Wheelchair Cannot Come Between Love," WBUR, "Here & Now," April 20, 2018, https://www.wbur.org/hereandnow/2018/04/20 /ben-mattlin-in-sickness-in-health (accessed June 10, 2019).

38. Now This, "Author Ben Matlin Gives an Intimate Take on Love in an Interabled Relationship," https://www.facebook.com/NowThisNews/videos /197501157868703/ (accessed June 10, 2019).

✆ Lesson 5: **All Means All**

What Ted and Josh Kuntz Taught Me

1. In memory of Josh Kuntz (1984–2017).

The Elephant in the Room Caroline Casey

2. Caroline Casey, "Looking Past Limits," TED Talk, April 8, 2011, https:// www.youtube.com/watch?v=YyBk55G7Keo.

3. Casey, "Looking Past Limits."

4. Denise Brodey, "This Woman Is Making Disability Inclusion a Leadership Issue," *Forbes*, https://www.forbes.com/sites/denisebrodey/2019/01/29/this-woman-is-making-disability-inclusion-a-leadership-issue/#7b90dcf21eac (accessed March 17, 2019).

5. Business Disability Forum, "Disability absent from leadership strategy in majority of global businesses," January 14, 2019, https://businessdisabilityforum.org.uk/media-centre/news/disability-absent-from-leadership-strategy/.

6. Caroline Casey, "We need to talk about disability inclusion," Comment Central, June 26, 2019, http://commentcentral.co.uk/we-need-to-talk-about-disability-inclusion/.

7. The Valuable 500, https://www.thevaluable500.com/.

8. The Valuable 500.

9. AdForum, *The Valuable 500—Diversish*, https://www.adforum.com/award-organization/6650183/showcase/2019/ad/34590323.

10. The Valuable 500.

Krip-Hop Nation Luca Patuelli

11. T'Cha Dunlevy, "For breakdance crew ILL-Abilities, physical challenges aren't crutches," February 14, 2019, *Montreal Gazette*, https://montrealgazette.com/entertainment/local-arts/skys-the-limit-for-ill-abilities-breakdance-crew (accessed June 1, 2019).

12. Colleen Connors, "'It's incredible': World-renowned b-boy Lazylegz breakdances in N.L.," CBC, https://www.cbc.ca/news/canada/newfoundland-labrador/it-s-incredible-world-renowned-b-boy-lazylegz-breakdances-in-n-l-1.4839420 (accessed June 1, 2019).

13. Judith Mackrell, "ILL-Abilities: The b-boy super crew taking on the able-bodied," *Guardian*, May 2, 2013, https://www.theguardian.com/stage/2013/may/02/ill-abilities-dance-breakin-convention (accessed June 1, 2019).

14. Mackrell, "ILL-Abilities."

15. Dunlevy, "For breakdance crew ILL-Abilities, physical challenges aren't crutches."

16. Dunlevy.

17. Luca "Lazylegz" Patuelli, "Life is a dance whether we know it or not," Creative Momentum, April 22, 2015, https://www.creativemoment.im/danceday message2015/ (accessed June 1, 2019).

18. Krip-Hop Nation, http://kriphopnation.com/.

Runway to the World Aaron Philip

19. @aaronphilipxo, Twitter, November 23, 2017, https://twitter.com/aaron philipxo/status/933901376278626304?lang=en.

20. Tyler Blint-Welsh, "A Path to the Runway, Paved With Hardship," *New York Times*, August 31, 2018, https://www.nytimes.com/2018/08/31/us/cerebral -palsy-transgender-fashion-model.html (accessed January 5, 2019).

21. Aaron Philip, "I'm a Black, Trans, Disabled Model—and I just Got Signed to a Major Agency," them., September 4, 2018, https://www.them.us /story/aaron-philip-signed-to-modeling-agency (accessed January 5, 2019).

22. Philip, "I'm a Black, Trans, Disabled Model."

23. Aaron Barksdale, "Trans Disabled Teen Model Aaron Philip Is the Future of Fashion," Vice, October 10, 2018, https://www.vice.com/en_ca/article/j53kp8 /trans-disabled-teen-model-aaron-philip-fashion.

24. D'Arcee Neal, "Meet the Disabled Trans Model Who's Here to DOMI-NATE the Fashion World," them., May 22, 2018, https://www.them.us/story /aaron-philip-fashion-and-disability (accessed January 5, 2019).

Unleash Different Rich Donovan

25. "The Walrus Talks Inclusion," May 7, 2019.

26. Rich Donovan, "A fresh approach to disability employment," BBC, "Ouch!" http://www.bbc.co.uk/ouch/opinion/disability-employment.shtml (accessed June 21, 2019).

27. "The Walrus Talks Inclusion."

28. "The Walrus Talks Inclusion."

Navigating Privilege and Power Deborah Dagit

29. Deborah Dagit, keynote speech, YouTube, April 8, 2015, https://www .youtube.com/watch?v=nnrqdB7zKLM.

30. Dagit, keynote speech.

31. Hector Perez, "Inspiring Story: Deb Dagit a Truly Inclusion Hero," Medium, December 3, 2018, https://medium.com/equapply/inspiring-story -deb-dagit-a-truly-inclusion-hero-c0b142ea3ddc (accessed April 24, 2019).

32. Dagit, keynote speech.

Sharing Lives The Village of Geel and Alex Fox

33. Karin Wells, "Psychiatric community care: Belgian town sets gold standard," CBC News, http://www.cbc.ca/news/world/psychiatric-community-care -belgian-town-sets-gold-standard-1.2557698 (accessed December 18, 2018).

34. WGBH, "Ah, My Brother" transcript, "Morning Stories," http://streams
.wgbh.org/online/morn/transcripts/MSPC20071130.pdf (accessed December 18,
2018).

35. Alex Fox, *A New Health and Care System: Escaping the Invisible Asylum*
(Bristol, UK: Policy Press, 2018).

An Authentic Doctor David Renaud

36. Stephen Letnes, "Able Artist Profile: David Renaud, MD," Able Artist
Foundation News, March 12, 2018, https://ableartist.org/article/able-artist
-profile-david-renaud-md (accessed January 15, 2019).

37. Letnes, "Able Artist Profile: David Renaud, MD."

38. Tara Bitran, "'Good Doctor' Writer David Renaud Aims at 'Authentic'
Depictions of People with Disabilities," *Variety*, September 23, 2018, https://
variety.com/2018/tv/features/david-renaud-good-doctor-disability-1202910405/
(accessed January 15, 2919).

All Means All Marsha Forest and Jack Pearpoint

39. Jack Pearpoint, personal correspondence with the author, January 2019.

40. Jack Pearpoint, personal conversation with the author, October 1, 2018.

❦ Lesson 6: **Adversity Is an Opportunity**

What Sam Sullivan Taught Me

1. *Sam Sullivan: Life in a Wheel*, Explore Films, 2009.

Mothering On Christa Couture

2. CBC Radio, "Christa Couture on love, loss and the power of music to
hold things together," "Unreserved," February 19, 2017, https://www.cbc.ca
/radio/unreserved/christa-couture-on-love-loss-and-the-power-of-music-to-hold
-things-together-1.3687546 (accessed November 19, 2018).

3. Louise Kinross, "Christa Couture sees beauty in resilience," Bloom, April
18, 2018, http://bloom-parentingkidswithdisabilities.blogspot.com/2018/04
/christa-couture-sees-beauty-in.html (accessed November 19, 2018).

4. Christa Couture, "That Time I Went Viral—for My Pregnancy Photos,"
Christa Couture, June 27, 2018, http://christacouture.com/that-time-i-went-viral
-for-my-pregnancy-photos/ (accessed November 19, 2018).

5. Christa Couture, "I don't just accept my disability—I can celebrate it,"
CBC Radio, "Tapestry," August 12, 2018, https://www.cbc.ca/radio/tapestry

/i-don-t-just-accept-my-disability-i-can-celebrate-it-1.4726383 (accessed November 19, 2018).

6. Christa Couture, "The M Word: Ever Since the End," *Christa Couture*, May 4, 2016, http://picklemethis.com/2016/05/01/the-m-word-ever-since-the-end-by -christa-couture/ (accessed November 19, 2018).

Breathing Love into Zika the *Guerreira* Mothers of Brazil

7. Katherine Jinyi Li, "Brazil's Zika mothers are speaking out," Seattle Globalist, June 28, 2016, https://www.seattleglobalist.com/2016/06/28/brazil-zika -mothers-speaking-out/53007.

8. William Kremer, "Zika Love Stories," BBC, https://www.bbc.co.uk/news /resources/idt-sh/zika_love_stories (accessed March 28, 2019).

9. Poonam Daryani, "Zika's Never-Ending Emergency," Pulitzer Center, February 26, 2018, https://pulitzercenter.org/reporting/zikas-never-ending -emergency.

Radical Optimist Helen Keller

10. Barbara Bindley, "Helen Keller—Why I Became an IWW," Industrial Workers of the World, originally published in the *New York Tribune*, January 15, 1916, https://www.iww.org/history/library/HKeller/why_I_became_an_IWW (accessed June 20, 2019).

11. Biography, "Helen Keller," https://www.biography.com/activist/helen -keller (accessed June 20, 2019).

12. Helen Keller, *Helen Keller's Journal: 1936–1937* (New York: Doubleday, Doran & Company, 1938).

13. Helen Keller, *The Story of My Life* (New York: W. W. Norton, 2003).

Adversity Is an Opportunity Aimee Mullins

14. Aimee Mullins, "The Opportunity of Adversity," TED Talk, October 2009, https://www.ted.com/talks/aimee_mullins_the_opportunity_of_adversity? language=en.

15. Mullins, "The Opportunity of Adversity."

16. Mullins.

Better and Darker Angels Abraham Lincoln

17. Joshua Wolf Shenk, "Lincoln's Great Depression," *Atlantic*, October 2005.

18. Shenk, "Lincoln's Great Depression."

19. Abraham Lincoln, Second Inaugural Address.

20. Lincoln, First Inaugural Address.

Image Maker Franklin Delano Roosevelt

21. fdr4freedoms, "I. Becoming a Leader: FDR Before the Presidency, 1882–1933," *http://fdr4freedoms.org/becoming-a-leader/* (accessed February 24, 2018).

22. Blanche Wiesen Cooke, *Eleanor Roosevelt: Volume 2, The Defining Years, 1933–1938* (New York: Penguin, 2000).

23. Naomi Klein, "A Message from the Future with Alexandria Ocasio-Cortez," Intercept, April 17, 2019, https://theintercept.com/2019/04/17/green-new-deal-short-film-alexandria-ocasio-cortez/ (accessed February 24, 2018).

24. Curtis Roosevelt, "FDR: A Giant Despite His Disability," *New York Times*, August 5, 1998, https://www.nytimes.com/1998/08/05/opinion/IHT-fdr-a-giant-despite-his-disability.html (accessed February 24, 2018).

25. Robert Graham, "Franklin Delano Roosevelt Memorial," http://www.robertgraham-artist.com/civic_monuments/fdr_memorial.html (accessed February 24, 2018).

Breaking Ground Pearl S. Buck

26. Stanley Finger and Shawn E. Christ, "Pearl S. Buck and Phenylketonuria (PKU)," *Journal of the History of the Neurosciences* 13, issue 1 (2004): 44–57.

27. Finger and Christ, "Pearl S. Buck and Phenylketonuria."

The Dark Side of the Game Tim Green

28. Brit McCandless Farmer, "Tim Green on His Emotional 60 Minutes Interview," *60 Minutes Overtime*, November 18, 2018, https://www.cbsnews.com/news/tim-green-als-emotional-60-minutes-interview/ (accessed February 3, 2019).

29. Tom Goldman, "Former NFL Player Tim Green Has a New Opponent—ALS," NPR, *Morning Edition*, December 12, 2018, https://www.npr.org/2018/12/12/675696565/former-nfl-player-tim-green-has-a-new-opponent-als (accessed February 3, 2019).

30. Goldman, "Former NFL Player Tim Green Has a New Opponent—ALS."

31. Goldman.

32. Steve Kroft, "Tim Green: Coping with the ALS He Thinks Was Caused by the Game He Loves," *60 Minutes*, https://www.cbsnews.com/news/tim-green-coping-with-the-als-he-thinks-was-caused-nfl-atlanta-falcons-syracuse-football-60-minutes/ (accessed February 3, 2019).

❦ Lesson 7: **Art Blooms at the Edges**

What Geoff McMurchy Taught Me

1. In memory of Geoff McMurchy (1955–2015).

Art Blooms at the Edges Yayoi Kusama

2. Yayoi Kusama, *Infinity Net: The Autobiography of Yayoi Kusama* (Chicago, IL: University of Chicago Press, 2012).

3. Kusama, *Infinity Net*.

4. Alexandra Munroe, "Yayoi Kusama at 90: How the 'undiscovered genius' became an international sensation," CNN, "Style," March 22, 2019, https://www.cnn.com/style/article/yayoi-kusama-artist/index.html (accessed June 5, 2019).

5. Priscilla Frank, "Selfie Obliteration: How Yayoi Kusama Invented the Photo-Friendly Art Show," HuffPost, October 21, 2015, https://www.huffington post.ca/entry/yayoi-kusama-selfies_n_562687ede4b08589ef493823 (accessed May 6, 2017).

6. Heather Lenz, director, *Kusama, Infinity*, documentary, 2018.

7. Lenz, *Kusama, Infinity*.

8. Lenz.

9. Ann Binlot, "Yayoi Kusama Contemplates Life and Death in Technicolor," *Daily Beast*, July 11, 2017, https://www.thedailybeast.com/yayoi-kusama -contemplates-life-and-death-in-technicolor (accessed June 27, 2019).

The Heart of the Matter Itzhak Perlman

10. Itzhak Perlman, "On Practicing," http://www.itzhakperlman.com/video/ (accessed May 31, 2018).

11. Alison Chernick, director, *Itzhak*, documentary, 2018, https://www.itzhak thefilm.com/.

12. Chernick, *Itzhak*.

13. Chernick.

14. Chernick.

15. Jack Riemer, "Perlman makes his music the hard way," *Houston Chronicle*, February 10, 2001, https://www.chron.com/life/houston-belief/article/Perlman -makes-his-music-the-hard-way-2009719.php (accessed May 31, 2018).

Black Beauty Anna Sewell

16. Anna Sewell, *Black Beauty: The Autobiography of a Horse* (New York: Penguin Random House, 2000).

17. Sewell, *Black Beauty*.

The Key of Life Stevie Wonder

18. Paul Lester, "I never thought of being blind and black as a disadvantage," *Guardian*, August 30, 2012, https://www.theguardian.com/music/2012/aug/30 /stevie-wonder-blind-black-disadvantage (accessed August 6, 2017).

19. Colleen Curry, "Stevie Wonder's Incredible History of Creating Change—on Stage and Off," Global Citizen, September 21, 2017, https://www .globalcitizen.org/en/content/stevie-wonders-history-of-creating-change-on-stage/ (accessed November 4, 2018).

20. Robert B. Black, "How Stevie Wonder Helped Create Martin Luther King Day," *BlackDoctor.org*, https://blackdoctor.org/477855/how-stevie-wonder-help -create-dr-king-holiday/ (accessed November 4, 2018).

21. Ambassadors for Peace, "Stevie Wonder, Ambassador for Peace," http:// ambassadorsforpeace.info/stevie-wonder-messenger-for-peace/ (accessed November 4, 2018).

A Chair in the Sky Charles Mingus with Joni Mitchell

22. Nat Hentoff, "Final Chorus: What About Mingus?" *JazzTimes*, December 1, 2008, https://jazztimes.com/features/columns/what-about-mingus/ (accessed June 2, 2019).

23. Leonard Feather, "Joni Mitchell Makes Mingus Sing," Joni Mitchell, originally published in *DownBeat*, September 6, 1979, https://jonimitchell.com /library/view.cfm?id=95 (accessed June 2, 2019).

24. Sue Graham Mingus, *Tonight at Noon: A Love Story* (Cambridge, MA: Da Capo Press, 2003).

Outsider Lucy Maud Montgomery

25. Margaret Atwood, "Nobody Ever Did Want Me," *Guardian*, March 28, 2008, https://www.theguardian.com/books/2008/mar/29/fiction.margaret atwood (accessed April 5, 2019).

26. Annette Lyon, "L. M. Montgomery and My Truth About Depression," Medium, March 13, 2018, https://medium.com/@annettelyon/l-m-montgomery -my-truth-about-depression-ecdf99ce6077 (accessed April 5, 2019).

27. Historica Canada, "Lucy Maud Montgomery," "Heritage Minutes," 2018, https://www.historicacanada.ca/content/heritage-minutes/lucy-maud -montgomery (accessed April 5, 2019).

28. Kate Macdonald Butler, "The heartbreaking truth about Anne's creator," *Globe and Mail*, September 20, 2008, https://www.theglobeandmail.com

/incoming/the-heartbreaking-truth-about-annes-creator/article17971607/ (accessed April 5, 2019).

Equals at Arthur's Round Table Niall McNeil and Marcus Youssef

29. Niall McNeil, personal conversation with the author, May 17, 2017.

30. Niall McNeil and Marcus Youssef, *King Arthur's Night and Peter Panties* (Vancouver, BC: Talonbooks, 2018).

31. McNeil and Youssef, *King Arthur's Night and Peter Panties*.

32. Becca Clarkson, "Vancouver Theatre Company to Take the Stage in Hong Kong," *Vancouver* magazine, January 15, 2019, http://vanmag.com/city/vancouver -theatre-company-to-take-the-stage-in-hong-kong/ (accessed February 1, 2019).

Changing the World, One Painting at a Time Yaniv Janson

33. Yaniv Daniel Janson, *Changing the World—One Painting at a Time* (Hamilton, New Zealand: Ecosynergy Creative, 2010).

34. Janson, *Changing the World*.

35. Yaniv Janson, *Please Do Touch*, Y-Artism Creative, New Zealand, 2017.

36. Yaniv Janson, blog, http://y-learning.blogspot.com/ (accessed August 6, 2018).

✃ Lesson 8: Awaken to All Your Senses

Touching the Rock John Hull

1. Mary D'Apice, "Interview with John Hull, Author of *Touching the Rock: An Experience of Blindness*," VisionAware, https://www.visionaware.org/info /emotional-support/personal-stories/eye-conditions-personal-stories/interview -with-john-hull-author-of-touching-the-rock-an-experience-of-blindness/1235 (accessed June 16, 2019).

2. D'Apice, "Interview with John Hull."

3. John Hull, *Touching the Rock: An Experience of Blindness* (New York: Pantheon Books, 1990).

4. John Hull, "Do You Think I'm Stupid?" JohnMHull.biz, http://www .johnmhull.biz/Do%20you%20think%20I%20am%20stupid.html.

5. Hull, *Touching the Rock*.

6. Saskia Baron, "How my husband saw blindness as a 'dark, paradoxical gift,'" Guardian, February 11, 2017, https://www.theguardian.com/lifeandstyle /2017/feb/11/john-hull-notes-on-blindness-wife-marilyn.

Awakening to Our Senses Evelyn Glennie

7. Evelyn Glennie, "What Makes Us Human," January 1, 2015, https://www
.evelyn.co.uk/what-makes-us-human/ (accessed June 28, 2018).

8. Glennie, "What Makes Us Human."

9. *Touch the Sound: A Sound Journey with Evelyn Glennie,* documentary, 2004.

10. Evelyn Glennie, "Hearing Essay," https://www.evelyn.co.uk/hearing
-essay/ (accessed June 28, 2018).

11. Katherine Ellison, "Tune In, Turn On," *Mindful,* July 29, 2016, https://
www.mindful.org/tune-in-turn-on/.

The Swoon of the Sensuous DJ Savarese

12. *Deej,* documentary, 2017, *https://www.deejmovie.com/.*

13. DJ Savarese, *A Doorknob for an Eye* (Unrestricted Editions, 2017).

14. *Deej,* https://www.deejmovie.com/poetry.

15. *Deej.*

The Sounds of Science Wanda Díaz-Merced

16. Wanda Díaz-Merced, "How a Blind Astronomer Found a Way to Hear
the Stars," TED Talk, February 2016.

17. Díaz-Merced, "How a Blind Astronomer Found a Way to Hear the Stars."

18. Star Songs, Harvard-Smithsonian Center for Astrophysics, https://www
.cfa.harvard.edu/sed/projects/star_songs/pages/xraytosound.html.

19. Wanda Díaz-Merced, "The Normalcy Curve," Women in Astronomy,
http://womeninastronomy.blogspot.com/2015/03/the-normalcy-curve.html
(accessed June 29, 2019).

Labyrinth Jorge Luis Borges

20. Patrick Kurp, "Review: Poems of the Night," *Quarterly Conversation,*
December 6, 2010, http://quarterlyconversation.com/poems-of-the-night-by
-jorge-luis-borges (accessed June 29, 2019).

21. Jorge Luis Borges, *Labyrinths* (New York: New Directions, 2007).

22. Shiv K. Kumar, "Conversations with Jorge Luis Borges, *Punch,* November
1, 2016, http://thepunchmagazine.com/the-byword/interviews/conversations
-with-jorge-luis-borges.

23. Jorge Luis Borges, "Blindness," 1977, https://www.gwern.net/docs
/borges/1977-borges-blindness.pdf (accessed June 29, 2019).

Transformer Man Neil Young

24. Neil Young, "Transformer Man," Genius, https://genius.com/Neil-young -transformer-man-lyrics.

25. Neil Young, MuchMusic TV interview, 1986, quoted in *Review of Disability Studies: An International Journal*, http://azrefs.org/review-of-disability-studies -an-international-journal.html?page=2.

26. Jimmy McDonough, *Shakey: Neil Young's Biography* (New York: Random House, 2002).

27. McDonough, *Shakey.*

28. Dangerous Minds, "Neil Young and Family Discuss Model Trains and His Son's Cerebral Palsy on Nickelodeon, 1994," February 5, 2015, http:// dangerousminds.net/comments/neil_young_family_discuss_model_trains (accessed June 3, 2019).

29. McDonough, *Shakey.*

In My Language Mel Baggs

30. Mel Baggs, YouTube, *In My Language*, YouTube, January 14, 2007, https://www.youtube.com/watch?v=JnylM1hI2jc.

31. Amanda Baggs, "Why we should listen to 'unusual' voices," *Anderson Cooper 360 Blog*, CNN, http://www.cnn.com/CNN/Programs/anderson.cooper .360/blog/2007/02/why-we-should-listen-to-unusual-voices.html (accessed June 30, 2019). (Amanda Baggs now goes by Mel Baggs.)

32. Baggs, "Why we should listen to 'unusual' voices."

A Little Learning Is a Dangerous Thing Alexander Pope

33. Alexander Pope, *The Works of Alexander Pope, Volume VI* (Farmington Hills, MI: Gale ECCO, 2010).

34. Lauren Riddell, "Alexander Pope: Grievous Disability and Inspired Writing," the cultural me, January 29, 2019, https://thecultural.me/alexander -pope-grievous-disability-and-inspired-writing-989986 (accessed June 3, 2019).

35. Riddell, "Alexander Pope."

36. Alexander Pope, "An Essay on Criticism," Poetry Foundation, https:// www.poetryfoundation.org/articles/69379/an-essay-on-criticism (accessed June 3, 2019).

By and for Equals Nadia Duguay and Exeko

37. Nadia Duguay and Agnès Lorgueilleux, "Fighting Social Exclusion, One Encounter at a Time," *Stanford Social Innovation Review*, Winter 2018, https://

ssir.org/articles/entry/fighting_social_exclusion_one_encounter_at_a_time (accessed June 28, 2019).

38. Exeko, https://exeko.org/en.

39. Exeko.

40. Exeko.

41. Duguay and Lorgueilleux, "Fighting Social Exclusion, One Encounter at a Time."

✆ Lesson 9: **Nothing about Us without Us**

What Barb Goode Taught Me

1. Barb Goode, *The Goode Life: Memoirs of Disability Rights Activist Barb Goode* (Vancouver, BC: Spectrum Press, 2011).

Climate Striking Greta Thunberg

2. John Sutter and Lawrence Davidson, "Teen tells climate negotiators they aren't mature enough," CNN, December 17, 2018, https://www.cnn.com/2018/12/16/world/greta-thunberg-cop24/index.html (accessed May 4, 2019).

3. Greta Thunberg, "We live in a strange world . . . ," New Story Hub, April 2, 2019, http://newstoryhub.com/2019/04/we-live-in-a-strange-world-greta-thunbergs-acceptance-speech-at-the-goldene-kamera-awards/ (accessed May 4, 2019).

4. Jonathan Watts, "Greta Thunberg, schoolgirl climate change warrior: 'Some people can let things go. I can't," March 11, 2019, *Guardian*, https://www.theguardian.com/world/2019/mar/11/greta-thunberg-schoolgirl-climate-change-warrior-some-people-can-let-things-go-i-cant (accessed May 4, 2019).

5. Greta Thunberg, Facebook, February 2, 2019, https://www.facebook.com/732846497083173/posts/767646880269801/ (accessed May 4, 2019).

6. Thunberg, Facebook.

Independent Living Ed Roberts

7. Victoria Dawson, "Ed Roberts' Wheelchair Records a Story of Obstacles Overcome," *Smithsonian*, March 13, 2015, https://www.smithsonianmag.com/smithsonian-institution/ed-roberts-wheelchair-records-story-obstacles-overcome-180954531/ (accessed May 8, 2019).

8. *Ed Roberts: Free Wheeling*, documentary, 1995, https://www.youtube.com/watch?v=ci3ek-tqiGQ.

9. ILUSA, *Ed Roberts, The Father of Independent Living,* https://www.ilusa.com/links/022301ed_roberts.htm (accessed May 8, 2019).

10. "About Ed: Ed Roberts Day 2018," YouTube, https://www.youtube.com/watch?v=KMYDoCr5lEg.

11. "About Ed: Ed Roberts Day 2018."

Accidental Activist Alice Wong

12. Melissa Hung, "The Most Damaging Way Movies Portray People with Disabilities," HuffPost, September 28, 2018, https://www.huffingtonpost.ca/entry/disability-media-movies-alice-wong_n_5bad0e22e4b0425e3c215d86 (accessed June 10, 2019).

13. Sarah Ruiz-Grossman, "You Don't Have to March to Be in the Resistance," HuffPost, May 25, 2017, https://www.huffingtonpost.ca/entry/disability-activism-resistance-alice-wong_n_59270f76e4b061d8f8201e8f (accessed June 10, 2019).

14. Nicola Griffith, "Resistance and Hope: An Interview with Alice Wong," October 16, 2018, https://nicolagriffith.com/2018/10/16/resistance-hope-an-interview-with-alice-wong/ (accessed June 10, 2019).

15. Ruiz-Grossman, "You Don't Have to March to Be in the Resistance."

16. Alice Wong, "Valuing Activism of All Kinds," Rooted in Rights, https://www.rootedinrights.org/valuing-activism-of-all-kinds/ (accessed June 10, 2019).

Manifesto for Citizenship Carmen Papalia

17. Carmen Papalia, "You Can Do It With Your Eyes Closed," *Art 21*, October 2014, http://magazine.art21.org/2014/10/07/you-can-do-it-with-your-eyes-closed/#.XRgOedNKhBw (accessed November 21, 2018).

18. Jacqueline Bell, "Practicing Accessibility: An Interview with Carmen Papalia," *Field*, issue 5 (Fall 2016), http://field-journal.com/issue-5/an-interview-with-carmen-papalia (accessed November 21, 2018).

19. Bell, "Practicing Accessibility."

Disability Rocks Heavy Load

20. "Disability Punk Band Heavy Load Says, Stay Up Late," Disabled World, editorial, July 15, 2009, https://www.disabled-world.com/editorials/heavy-load.php (accessed January 13, 2019).

21. Alexis Petridis, "We Played Mencap and they told us to turn it down," *Guardian*, https://www.theguardian.com/music/2008/sep/13/popandrock.musicdocumentary (accessed January 13, 2019).

22. PaulR, "A manifesto for an ordinary life," Stay Up Late, December 14, 2018, https://stayuplate.org/a-manifesto-for-an-ordinary-life/ (accessed January 13, 2019).

The Equality Effect Fiona Sampson

23. *Gazette*, "Dr. Fiona Sampson on her career, the importance of human rights advocacy, and the possibilities of justice for women," Law Society of Ontario, http://www.lawsocietygazette.ca/news/dr-fiona-sampson-on-her-career-the-importance-of-human-rights-advocacy-and-the-possibilities-of-justice-for-women/ (accessed June 10, 2019).

24. Queen's Alumni, "QUAA Alumni Humanitarian Award recipient uses human rights law to protect 10 million Kenyan girls," March 8, 2016, https://www.queensu.ca/alumni/news/quaa-alumni-humanitarian-award-recipient-uses-human-rights-law-to-protect-10-million-kenyan-girls (accessed June 10, 2019).

25. Sally Armstrong, "Kenyan's girls' quest for justice realized, with Canadian help," *Star*, March 12, 2017, https://www.thestar.com/news/insight/2017/03/12/kenyan-girls-quest-for-justice-realized-with-canadian-help.html (accessed June 10, 2019).

26. David Bruser, "Thalidomide victims say federal government has broken promises of 'full' support," *Star*, December 5, 2017, https://www.thestar.com/news/canada/2017/12/05/thalidomide-victims-say-federal-government-has-broken-promises-of-full-support.html.

27. Kristy Kirkup, "Thalidomide survivor calls on government to boost annual payment," National Newswatch, January 10, 2019, https://www.nationalnewswatch.com/2019/01/10/thalidomide-survivor-calls-on-government-to-boost-annual-payment/#.XUyThdNKhBw.

28. "Fiona Sampson, the Equality Effect and the Global Summit to End Sexual Violence in Conflict: Translating Rhetoric to Action," *Global Justice Center Blog*, July 1, 2014, http://globaljusticecenter.net/blog/400-fiona-sampson-the-equality-effect-and-the-global-summit-to-end-sexual-violence-in-conflict-translating-rhetoric-to-action (accessed June 10, 2019).

Breaking Bad Barriers RJ Mitte

29. Travis M. Andrews, "'Not much has changed': Actress Marlee Matlin on Hollywood's portrayal of people with disabilities," *Washington Post*, February 27, 2017, https://www.washingtonpost.com/news/morning-mix/wp/2017/02/27

/not-much-has-changed-actress-marlee-matlin-on-the-representation-of-the
-disabled-in-hollywood/.

30. Karen Brill, "A New Study Says 95 Percent of Actors Playing Disabled
Characters on TV Are Able-Bodied," Vulture, July 13, 2016, https://www.vulture
.com/2016/07/tv-has-very-few-disabled-actors-study-says.html (accessed Jun 26,
2019).

31. Andrews, "Not much has changed."

32. Pippa Raga, "Bryan Cranston's 'Breaking Bad' Co-Star RJ Mitte Weighs
in on 'The Upside' Controversy," *Distractify, 2019*, https://www.distractify.com
/trending/2019/01/18/J2CpCm0u2/new-bryan-cranston-movie-disability
(accessed Jun 26, 2019).

33. Jane Mulkerrins, "RJ Mitte: A disabled actor should be free to audition
for a non-disabled role," *Evening Standard*, January 29, 2016, https://www
.standard.co.uk/lifestyle/london-life/rj-mitte-a-disabled-actor-should-be-free-to
-audition-for-a-nondisabled-role-a3168141.html (accessed June 26, 2019).

34. Nic Cha Kim, "Breaking Bad Actor Makes Good for Diversity in Hollywood," Spectrum News 1, https://spectrumnews1.com/ca/la-west/news/2019/04
/25/disability-is-diversity?cid=twitter_SpecNews1SoCal# (accessed Jun 26, 2019).

35. Kim, "Breaking Bad Actor Makes Good for Diversity in Hollywood."

Everything Is about Us Carla Qualtrough

36. CBC Radio, "Minister Carla Qualtrough says Canada's new disability
act will make history," "Current," October 21, 2016, https://www.cbc.ca/radio
/thecurrent/a-special-edition-of-the-current-focused-on-disability-for-october-21
-2016-1.3814141/minister-carla-qualtrough-says-canada-s-new-disability-act-will
-make-history-1.3814165 (accessed October 31, 2018).

37. Paralympic.org, "Big Interview: The Honourable Carla Qualtrough,"
April 26, 2017, https://www.paralympic.org/news/big-interview-honourable
-carla-qualtrough (accessed October 31, 2018).

38. OpenParliament.ca, transcript of Bill C-81, "An Act to ensure a barrier-
free Canada," November 21, 2018, https://openparliament.ca/debates/2018/11
/21/carla-qualtrough-2/ (accessed November 22, 2018).

Did You Know . . .

39. Office of the Governor, Greg Abbott, "Disability History Factoid:
October 14, 2011, Stephen Hopkins," https://content.govdelivery.com/accounts
/TXGOV/bulletins/15e4d2 (accessed June 1, 2019).

40. John Milton, "On His Blindness," Bartleby.com, https://www.bartleby
.com/101/318.html (accessed May 4, 2018).

ॐ Lesson 10: **There Is No Independence without Interdependence**

Becoming Human Jean Vanier

1. Roy Bonisteel, host, "Man Alive: Jean Vanier," CBC, April 9, 1973, https://
www.cbc.ca/archives/entry/man-alive-jean-vanier (accessed June 29, 2019).

2. Jean Vanier, *Seeing Beyond Depression* (Mahwah, NJ: Paulist Press, 2001).

3. Krista Tippett, "The Tender Power of Jean Vanier," On Being, May 7, 2019,
https://onbeing.org/blog/the-tender-power-of-jean-vanier/ (accessed June 29,
2019).

4. Jean Vanier, *Becoming Human* (Toronto, Canada: House of Anansi Press,
2008).

5. Jean Vanier, *Community and Growth* (London, UK: Darton, Longman &
Todd, 2006).

6. Jean Vanier, *From Brokenness to Community* (Mahwah, NJ: Paulist Press,
1982), 23.

Love's Labor Eva Kittay

7. Webteam, interview with Eva Feder Kittay, Ethics of Care, June 16, 2013,
https://ethicsofcare.org/eva-fedar-kittay/ (accessed July 14, 2019).

8. Eva Feder Kittay, *Love's Labor: Essays on Women, Equality and Dependency*
(New York: Routledge, 1998).

9. Eva Kittay, "Love's Labor Revisited," *Hypatia* 17, no. 3 (Summer 2002),
http://evafederkittay.com/wp-content/uploads/2015/01/loves-labor-revisited.pdf
(accessed June 14, 2019).

Purple, Green, and Yellow Robert Munsch

10. Robert Munsch, https://robertmunsch.com/about.

11. Ann Hui, "The Backstory," *Walrus*, November 12, 2010, https://thewalrus
ca/the-backstory/ (accessed April 15, 2019).

12. André Picard, "How Robert Munsch grabbed a lifeline," *Globe and Mail*,
October 9, 2009, https://www.theglobeandmail.com/life/health-and-fitness
/health/conditions/how-robert-munsch-grabbed-a-lifeline/article4268136/
(accessed April 15, 2019).

13. Mental Health Commission of Canada, "Robert Munsch speaks about mental health," https://www.mentalhealthcommission.ca/English/media/1690 (accessed April 15, 2019).

Moonbeams Ian Brown

14. Ian Brown, *The Boy in the Moon: A Father's Journey to Understand His Extraordinary Son* (New York: St. Martin's Press, 2009).
15. Brown, *The Boy in the Moon.*
16. Brown.
17. Brown.

The Four Walls of Her Freedom Donna Thomson

18. Geraldine Bedell, "My life as a carer, by a diplomat's wife," *The Times,* September 7, 2010, https://www.thetimes.co.uk/article/my-life-as-a-carer-by-a -diplomats-wife-6zlzqb2gn5t#%23 (accessed July 27, 2017).
19. Bedell, "My life as a carer, by a diplomat's wife."
20. Donna Thomson, *The Four Walls of My Freedom: Lessons I've Learned From a Life of Caregiving* (Toronto, Canada: House of Anansi Press, 2014).
21. Thomson, *The Four Walls of My Freedom.*
22. Donna Thomson, "So That's It! How to Be Happy," *Caregivers' Living Room,* August 1, 2015, https://www.donnathomson.com/2015/08/so-thats-it-how -to-be-happy.html.

The Untouchables Philippe Pozzo di Borgo and Abdel Sellou

23. Sabine Oelze, "Quadriplegic: 'Weakness is a treasure,'" DW, March 14, 2013, https://www.dw.com/en/quadriplegic-weakness-is-a-treasure/a-16672926 (accessed May 1, 2019).
24. Oelze, "Quadriplegic."
25. Oelze.
26. Abdel Sellou, *You Changed My Life: A Memoir* (New York: Weinstein Books, 2012).
27. Philippe Pozzo di Borgo, *A Second Wind: A Memoir* (New York: Atria Books, 2018), 105.

Poem for Michael Kirsteen Main

28. Kirsteen Main, *Dear Butterfly: 50 Poems,* 2014, used with permission, https://planinstitute.ca/learning-centre/publications/dear-butterfly/.
29. Main, *Dear Butterfly,* 45.

There Is No Independence without
Interdependence Bonnie Sherr Klein

30. Bonnie Sherr Klein, *Slow Dance: A Story of Stroke, Love, and Disability* (Toronto, Canada: Knopf Canada, 1997).

31. Tim Adams, "Naomi Klein: Trump is an idiot, but don't underestimate how good he is at that," *Guardian*, June 11, 2017, https://www.theguardian.com/books/2017/jun/11/naomi-klein-donald-trump-no-is-not-enough-interview (accessed July 20, 2018).

32. Adams, "Naomi Klein."

33. Naomi Klein, "Occupy Wall Street: The Most Important Thing in the World Now," *Nation*, October 6, 2011, https://www.thenation.com/article/occupy-wall-street-most-important-thing-world-now/ (accessed July 20, 2018).

34. National Film Board, *Shameless: The ART of Disability*, written and directed by Bonnie Sherr Klein, 2006, available free from the NFB.

Thanks

TO ALL THE people I wrote about: I spent days getting to know each of you, absorbing everything I could find. Your profile does not do you justice and it's much too short. I apologize for any inaccuracies and will correct them in subsequent editions. I sincerely hope it makes people curious to find out more about you and your work. Special appreciation to Marlena Blavin, Caroline Casey, Christa Couture, Nadia Duguay, Catherine Frazee, Barb Goode, Annick Janson, Bonnie Sherr Klein, Ted Kuntz, Victoria Maxwell, Carmen Papalia, Jack Pearpoint, David Roche, Sam Sullivan, Donna Thomson, Alice Wong, Ing Wong-Ward, and Marcus Youssef for your clarifications.

To Vickie Cammack, Deborah Dagit, Rich Donovan, Tracey Friesen, Steve Hanamura, and Michael Harling for reviewing various drafts of the manuscript. This book is so much better because of you.

To Kirsteen Main for permission to use her poem.

To Pamela Cushing, Aaron Johannes, Roger Jones, Tim Louis, Ken LaHaie, Yazmine Laroche, Penny Parry, Lauren Stinson, and Natalie Wright for your encouragement and advice. Especially to Paul Born, Michael Harling, Bonnie Sherr Klein, and Marcus Youssef for your extra support.

To Jacques Dufresne for your friendship and wisdom.

To Steve Piersanti for his editing, confidence, and encouragement. You and the Berrett-Koehler team really are a writer's best friend.

To Cindy Hughes for her photograph.

To Liz for the education and love. I look forward to going on the road with you and this book. If you are not too busy.

Finally, to my wife, Vickie Cammack, for your edits, feedback, and significant contributions to this book, in particular "There Is No Independence without Interdependence." And as always for the great meals, laughter, and love. I delight in your presence.

About the Author

AL ETMANSKI is a community organizer, social entrepreneur, and writer. He is an Ashoka social enterprise fellow and a member of John McKnight's Asset-Based Community Development (ABCD) network. He became a parent activist in the disability movement after his daughter Liz was born. Liz was the first person with Down syndrome to graduate from Emily Carr University of Art and Design. She is now a full-time artist and occasional poet.

Al led the closure of large institutions that warehoused people with developmental disabilities in his home province of British Columbia and helped close segregated schools and integrate students with disabilities into regular classrooms. He was behind a successful Supreme Court judgment that secured the right to treatment for a young boy who a lower court had determined was too disabled to feel any pain and should be left to die. The case established a legal precedent. He also helped establish Canada's first Family Support Institute and a grassroots alternative to costly and intrusive legal guardianship.

In 1989, he cofounded Planned Lifetime Advocacy Network (PLAN) along with his wife, Vickie Cammack. PLAN was developed to help people with disabilities to live a good life, particularly after the parents die. They didn't realize it at the time, but it is the first time in history that a generation of people with disabilities are outliving their parents, and governments and service providers are not prepared. PLAN facilitates a network of friends for individuals and maximizes their financial resources. It also works at the policy level to eliminate the poverty and social isolation experienced by too many people with disabilities. The PLAN approach has spread to more than forty locations around the world. While at PLAN, Al proposed and led the campaign to create the world's first savings plan for people with disabilities, the Registered Disability Savings Plan (RDSP), in 2008. The collective RDSP deposits total more than $4 billion, benefiting close to two hundred thousand Canadians with disabilities. The money can be used on whatever the individual chooses, can't be clawed back, and doesn't have to be reported.

Fifteen years ago, Al left PLAN to immerse himself in the emerging field of social innovation. He wanted to understand why so many of his initiatives started with a big splash and seemed to be successful, but in the long term they barely made a difference. He became part of a countrywide initiative to introduce concepts of social innovation and social finance to Canadian changemakers. His last book, *Impact: Six Patterns to Spread Your Social Innovation*, highlights six deep patterns of change making that he observed groups using to close the gap between short-term success and long-term structural and cultural impact.

Al believes that extraordinary acts are not reserved for the special few and that everyone's actions are important to make a world that works for everyone. He is optimistic about what we can do together. He says that magnificence occurs when we sprinkle our work with beauty and love.

He has received numerous awards, including the Order of Canada, the Order of British Columbia, and the Big Picture award from his peers in the disability movement.

Al and Vickie have a blended family of five children. *The Power of Disability* is his fourth book. He blogs at www.aletmanski.com.

Dear reader,

Thank you for picking up this book and welcome to the worldwide BK community! You're joining a special group of people who have come together to create positive change in their lives, organizations, and communities.

What's BK all about?

Our mission is to connect people and ideas to create a world that works for all.

Why? Our communities, organizations, and lives get bogged down by old paradigms of self-interest, exclusion, hierarchy, and privilege. But we believe that can change. That's why we seek the leading experts on these challenges—and share their actionable ideas with you.

A welcome gift

To help you get started, we'd like to offer you a **free copy** of one of our bestselling ebooks:

www.bkconnection.com/welcome

When you claim your **free ebook**, you'll also be subscribed to our blog.

Our freshest insights

Access the best new tools and ideas for leaders at all levels on our blog at ideas.bkconnection.com.

Sincerely,

Your friends at Berrett-Koehler

Certified

Corporation